Meritage DIV♥RCE

" A BLEND OF FINANCIAL, PHYSICAL, EMOTIONAL, AND SPIRITUAL GUIDANCE
...THROUGH **WINE** COLORED GLASSES."

**by
Cheryl Nielsen**

Lissa,

Cheers!

Cheryl Nielsen

Meritage Divorce: A blend of financial, physical, emotional, and spiritual guidance...through wine colored glasses

Copyright © 2012 by Cheryl Nielsen

For media inquiries and special discounts for bulk purchases please contact:
Cheryl@meritagedivorce.com

www.meritagedivorce.com

Logo & Cover design: Angie Pines, pureprassociates.com

Digital book(s) (epub and mobi) produced by: Booknook.biz

To all those in the midst of divorce...

Your journey will have seasons just as a vineyard. All seasons have their purpose.

Embrace the journey as it will birth the fruit of your soul.

It was a Jordan Cabernet Sauvignon that stole my palate and made a wine lover out of me. I drank it for the first time on my honeymoon in 1995. I'm not sure of the vintage, but I recall the experience. It awakened my wine palate and is responsible for the wino I am today.

I'd like to thank Jordan Vineyard & Winery for the exceptional wines I have enjoyed over the years and extend heartfelt thanks for contributing the video links to pair with some of my writing. I am most appreciative.

You can visit Jordan Vineyard & Winery at www.jordanwinery.com.

I'd like to introduce the first video:

Cabernet Sauvignon Veraison in Alexander Valley

http://www.bit.ly/jordancab

Veraison is the changing color of green grapes to red when sugar accumulation begins and acids decrease.

TABLE OF TASTINGS

Meritage

DIV♥RCE

" A BLEND OF FINANCIAL, PHYSICAL, EMOTIONAL, AND SPIRITUAL GUIDANCE
...THROUGH **WINE** COLORED GLASSES."

YOU'VE GOT SOMETHING TO WINE ABOUT

"There are two things you should never do alone: one is get divorced, the other is drink."

Cheryl Nielsen

You're getting divorced. It's okay—go ahead and wine about it. You might feel better. This book is written for you and the wining is included. I don't want anyone going through divorce to do it alone. We can do this together—the divorce and the drinking in moderation, of course.

Books, wine, dogs, a few friends, and a vineyard were my constant companions throughout my divorce. More often than not, however, I was alone—drinking wine and working in the vineyard. The dogs watched me grieve. I poured myself into my work while I tried to spit out the past, re-produce myself, and decant a future. I thought I was living life through wine-colored glasses—the ones you can see through with the most clarity—and I thought I was alone; yet, neither turned out to be the case.

If we have God and ourselves, are we really alone? I think not. We can also ask ourselves: Does God want us to drink wine? The answer is: of course! Otherwise, he wouldn't have created grapes. And if you like wine as much as I do, you can conclude: "There is a God." So, in my mind, wine makes the world go around. I also believe that God knew it wasn't going to be a per-fect world when he made man and woman so different and asked them to understand each other and blend together in matrimony to become one in harmony. When paired well with another, you compliment; paired incorrectly, the aftertaste will sneak up on you. One thing was for sure: God didn't forget me. The Master Winemaker had a vision for the wine he wanted me to become and a winemaking plan to get me there. It was up to me to buy into the plan or not.

God knew I was deeply unhappy and in need of changing my life. He wanted me to live a more purposeful life, with love and joy. He needed to soften the tannins of my backbone, and give me some additional maturity and complex characteristics to prepare me for the happy life ahead of me. I was released on the other side of divorce with a burning desire to share some of the wisdom of my experience and give hope, support, companionship, and guidance to those of you who are embarking on this tumultuous journey, and to tell you that you really can get something positive out of the experience. You may not be able to escape the pain, but you can use divorce as a refinement process that gives you a better version of yourself than the one you had before—a more drinkable one. Always remember: things happen for a reason—even if that reason isn't apparent at the time.

People also come into our lives for a reason just as they leave for a reason. Should I drink the wine of a marriage blend with a bitter aftertaste indefinitely to avoid becoming a divorce statistic and presumed failure? No. I would be crazy to keep drinking only to expect a different taste to result. I do not equate divorce with failure. Perhaps as you mature, your taste changes as wine does when it ages. What once blended well no longer compliments the other and the two of you paired have aged into a concoction that you no longer recognize or have a taste for. There are many other reasons for not labeling divorce as a failure.

How can your life experience that helped you evolve and provided you with wisdom ever be deemed a failure? The marriage delivered something of great value at one time. There are parting gifts that will forever be yours such as your personal growth, good memories, the children, and experiences that helped shape who you are today. These gifts don't get returned. They are yours to keep forever.

We are going to take a Meritage Divorce journey laced with wine and vineyard metaphors as you transition and embark on self-discovery and ultimately earn your wine-colored glasses. Are you ready? Do you want to see with better clarity and use this time to re-produce yourself and become the wine you are meant to be? If the answer is "Yes," let's get started!

The word Meritage is indicative to blended wine. The word is also a wine designation used to describe a blend of two or more Bordeaux grape varietals grown on non-French soil. Meritage is pronounced MEHR-ih-tij in the wine world. In the divorce world, I pronounce it meh-rih-Taagghhhe with no disrespect to the French or Meritage Association for my seeming ignorant.

A Meritage wine gets its complexity and character from the winemaker's craftsmanship and carefully selected varietals of varying proportions, which blend together to deliver its unique taste, aroma, color, and other characteristics. The key is in the blend. This finished product is the sum of its parts. Each varietal relies on the other to play its role in delivering its unique qualities to yield a one-of-a-kind experience. The wines act in a partnership, of sorts. Sound familiar?

You might be asking yourself, how does a Meritage wine relate to divorce? A Meritage Divorce is a blend of financial, physical, emotional, and spiritual guidance. These areas represent the interdependent parts of one's collective life experience. Each relies on the other to do its part. Just like the winemaker, you are responsible for blending these areas together to deliver your one-of-a-kind experience. There will be much change and growth in these areas as you work through your transition to find your perfect blend. Stay adaptable to change; keep an open mind; don't be afraid to let go of old beliefs and embrace new learning. Free up your mind to new experiences.

Some of the guidance to support you with your transition and personal growth will be contained within the pages of this book from my personal experience, journal exercises, and professionals you choose for your divorce support system. Other guidance may come when you least suspect it. Answers may arrive to you through epiphanies as new realities surface and are realized. Trust your instincts. You are going to become the winemaker of who you want to become. If you trust the process, you will re-produce yourself and deliver the new you on the other side of the journey.

In the process, try on a few shades of wine-colored glasses and see if you like the way they fit: golden yellows of

Chardonnay, burgundy hues for those delicious varietals like Cabernet Sauvignon, Zinfandel, and Pinot Noir to name a few. We'll try them all until you find a pair that fits and you can see perfectly out of them. Throw the rose-colored glasses out and make way for the wine-colored glasses—you'll be able to see with greater clarity. Sound like a journey worth taking? I hope you join me.

Cheers! — Cheryl Nielsen

MERITAGE DIVORCE WINE DEFINITIONS

"I speak three languages: one is English, one is divorce, and the other is wine, sometimes in the same sentence."

Cheryl Nielsen

Before we take this journey, you will need to become familiar with some of the wine terms and definitions that are used throughout the book. Some you may already be familiar with, while others you never needed to concern yourself with to enjoy a glass of wine. Yet other wine terms, I defined with my own agenda in mind. Either way, you'll need to get the wine lingo down to get the message I am trying to convey.

I also poke fun at some types of wine. Please forgive me; there really isn't a bad type, it is a matter of personal taste and what appeals to your palate. So here they are:

Aftertaste: The taste or flavors that linger in the mouth after the wine is tasted, spit, or swallowed. Also referred to as the "finish"— important when considering the wine's character and quality.

Backbone: The backbone of a wine is what gives structure and holds its various elements together—provided by the acidity or tannins.

Barrel Refinement Process: Adopted and re-defined from "Malolactic Fermentation," which is a secondary fermentation that converts the naturally occurring Malic acid into Lactic acid.

This can result in a "creamy" or "buttery" texture in Chardonnays, for example. Also referred to as being "re-produced" in Meritage Divorce.

Blend or Blended: Any two wines blended together in a marriage or relationship.

Blending: Wines that blend with more than one varietal.

Body: The viscosity or thickness of wine. The higher the alcohol, the more full-bodied the wine.

Bouquet: The fragrance or aroma of a wine.

Corked: Wine that doesn't taste right as a result of a tainted cork.

Cab: The name I've given my ex-husband in the book (short for Cabernet Sauvignon).

Character: Distinctive taste characteristics describing a wine.

Charm: A wine that is balanced in pleasing elements with nothing that stands out more than the other.

Cigar Box: Refers to the essence of cedar and tobacco aroma associated with mature Cabernet Sauvignon and Cabernet blends.

Decant: Allowing wine to breathe or open up.

Ex-wine: An ex-spouse or person previously in a blended relationship.

Hallow: A tasting experience that is lacking between the first taste and the finish.

Hot: A wine that is high in alcohol.

Length: Describes how long the flavor of the wine lingers on the palate after swallowing.

Malolactic fermentation: See "Barrel Refinement Process."

Mature: Describes a more drinkable wine as measured by the wine's readiness to drink. Not the same as its age.

Mouthfeel: How a wine feels in the mouth and against the tongue.

Palate: Refers to the overall experience with wine including the taste and feel in your mouth and after it has been swallowed.

Re-produced: See "Barrel Refinement Process."

Skin: The skin of the grape gives the wine flavor and color.

Sediments: Small particles in wine from the grape skins, seeds, and other grape particles that settle at the bottom of the bottle. They are bitter when tasted.

Tannins: Naturally occurring in wines from skins, seeds, and stems. They are a bitter component used to balance the wine. Not good if out of balance.

Tasting Appointments: Any time spent in the company of wine similar to wine tasting.

Tasting Notes: Evaluation of a wine in terms of color or appearance, bouquet and taste.

Tight: Describes a wine's structure or body as in "tightly wound" wine.

Varietal: An adjective used to describe wine made from a certain variety of grape. "Merlot" is an example of a varietal.

Vintage: The vintage refers to the year the grapes were grown.

Young: Wine that is not matured—not its age but refers to drinkability.

In the wine world, there are many descriptors and technical terms. One needs not to get too caught up in this to describe wine. Winemaker Rob Davis of Jordan Winery learns this lesson in this video:

Learning How to Taste Wine with Winemaker André Tchelistcheff

http://www.bit.ly/jordanwinetasting

Immediately after graduating from UC-Davis in 1976, Winemaker Rob Davis accepted a winemaking position at Jordan Winery, excited about the opportunity to apprentice under a California winemaking legend hired by the Jordan family as consulting enologist: André Tchelistcheff. In this charming story, Rob recollects how André taught him to think beyond the traditional winemaking descriptions and start assessing wine passionately rather than scientifically.

THE MOMENT OF TRUTH

"This sublime nectar is quite simply incapable of lying. Picked well or picked too late, it matters not, the wine will always whisper in your mouth unabashed honesty every time you take a sip."

Albert Finney delivered this line in the movie *A Good Year*

Before we begin, you need to ask yourself: Have you been drinking bad wine? When I chose my husband, Cab, for marriage he was like a young wine—full of potential, but not yet fully matured. I thought he was the right varietal for me, a Cabernet Sauvignon that would, over time, become more refined, confident, and smooth on the palate. But, as time went by, I realized he was more and more like a Cabernet, but not in the ways I anticipated. Yes, he showed outward signs of sophistication and complex characteristics and, truth be told, he was somewhat full bodied; however, he was anything but smooth on my palate. In the beginning, to my fairly inexperienced palate, he was wonderful—he tasted great, and at least I thought he was just the type of wine that I liked, but sometime during our fifteen-year relationship he had corked.

Before I knew it, my beautiful wine, the wine that I took so long to select, had turned rancid on the palate. Sarcasm was his primary form of expression. As time went by, he became harder and harder to swallow. He wasn't the smooth, velvety wine I thought I'd selected. No, he was sour with a bitter aftertaste. Everything about our situation sickened my stomach and made me nauseated. What I once anticipated in the form of a loving relationship did not deliver the experience I had hoped for. I wanted to be drank with appreciation and cherished. I longed for some written, heartfelt, tasting notes of the things he enjoyed and appreciated about me. Instead, the notes were more critical in nature and delivered verbally sarcastic.

There were times, of course, when I could taste the essence of the original uncorked wine camouflaged under the layers of acidity. There were even times I told myself: Maybe he's really not corked; maybe it's me. Maybe it's my palate and the way I perceive the experience. After all, taste is subjective. Perhaps I was contributing in some way to the experience I was having. Maybe I needed to clean my palate and come to the table without the typical schemas we develop over time in relation to our spouses. These preconceived notions I had were based on a set of patterns that had played out over and over again so many times I could almost anticipate the outcome. The problem was that over time, my palate became more and more sophisticated—I knew the difference between good wine and bad wine, and once you know the difference, you don't want to drink the bad stuff anymore.

In the beginning, I was a white zinfandel, which I consider to be a wannabe wine. I came to the marriage naïve. I lacked confidence and didn't recognize my potential. I was fairly sweet on the palate initially. I tried to keep the relationship easy to swallow by not asking for too much. I earned my own money and contributed equally financially while taking a backseat to lifestyle opportunities. Instead, I worked around the clock and did little to enjoy the simple pleasures in life. Through self-discovery later, I would come to understand why.

Having drunk the nectar of only a few wines prior, I certainly did not have a finely tuned palate to know what I liked nor what would be a good blend for me. I did know I was eager to build a future with someone and to be loved. The two of us together, as a blended wine, did little to complement each other or provide the right balance. Ideally, and if they're properly blended, two varietals can be a better-finished product than each on their own. Together, their characteristics should complement, enhance, and support the other to make each better than they are alone.

We were mismatched from the beginning. Neither of us could deliver to the other what we needed to flourish, grow, or nurture each other properly to help each other reach our potential or feel loved. Neither one of us inherently showed love to each other in the way we could feel it. I needed love demonstrated to me with acts of service, such as being proactive in maintaining my car or some aspect of our home, and words of affirmation as in the words behind "I love you," telling me why. I got tired of those three words. They were like empty calories; they needed action behind them. They felt like a lazy way of expressing love.

Cab believed in hiring out most services. He once told me that he made sure his share of household chores were done—even if by others—therefore, they were performed and if he paid for them, he should get credit for them. Good thing the spa guy wasn't that cute or I might have fallen in love with him for performing acts of service for me.

Cab told me he needed to feel love through affection. I could have hired that one out too, but I didn't want to go to jail. Even though it would have been a physical manifestation of the emotional prison I felt I was living in. I didn't feel like touching him after a sarcastic comment. I retreated emotionally and love slipped slowly out of my heart. He didn't get the affection he needed to feel loved either. It was a vicious cycle.

But there was at least one common characteristic that held us together. We were both very ambitious and had a desire to be financially well-off and able to afford the finer things in life. I was running from the feeling I had growing up of not feeling my family was financially secure.

It took years of hard work to become financially well-off and I believe we sacrificed our relationship in the process. I had transitioned out of corporate America after five years as a Human Resources Manager into self-employment as a Real Estate Broker. I had a very driven, independent mind-set. Failure was not an option. I had a strong work ethic to a fault. I didn't take care of myself or acknowledge my needs or Cabs. I was hell-bent on not needing anyone. I had never been able to count on anyone in my life and I wasn't going to start now was my attitude. We were both good at growing our businesses and a small empire of financial assets, but we were not good at keeping our marriage alive and healthy. The marriage seemed like another item on the list of to-dos.

As Cab's financial planning business grew, he took on a partner and other strategic business partners and a "boys club" was born. It was as though there was a sign at the office—naked to the human eye—but the message was loud and clear and it read: "no wives allowed." It got to the point that if I wanted to talk about something financial, I had to make an appointment with Cab's assistant to come to the office and discuss the matter.

The boys knew how to live too. They enjoyed a lifestyle of golf trips, fine dining, and expensive wine. I did enjoy the "doggie-bag" boxed leftovers, however, and occasionally it was a bonus when one or more of the boys had leftovers too. Steak bones were a common treat for the dogs. The dogs and I ate well— ruff, ruff. I felt like I was under the table like a dog on its hind legs with my mouth open waiting to be fed—no longer invited to the table—just good enough to eat the scraps.

The boys came over for dinner with their wives and I cooked for them—course dinners with paired wine, complete with a well-dressed table and candles. Kind of ironic that I was so busy preparing the meal and serving it I was once again on the outside looking in and not at the table. Sometimes I sat in the back seat of the car while one of the "boys" sat in the front. I felt like I had become a second wife. The business and friends came first. I was a mere leftover thought—no left overs intended.

Silence was common in our house. Communication became painful. The sarcasm was a piercing sword to my heart. The tongue was our biggest weapon—giving opportunity to inflict emotional pain. The reaction I gave to the sarcasm was defensive verbally and my voice got louder and louder over time. I became chronically tired. The enthusiasm for life was nonexistent.

As life got more sophisticated and lifestyles increased, our egos got bigger too. We had built several businesses and managed investment properties. We both entertained clients and friends— wining and dining was a way of life. As the years went on, the pressure to manage all that we had acquired consumed our energies. We had little energy left to put toward fixing the relationship. With each subsequent year, the emotional deposits were smaller and smaller until I was overdrawn and emotionally bankrupt. I no longer had the emotional reserves to weather the challenges in the relationship or to participate emotionally in it.

In the first half of our marriage, I received my words of affirmation in cards for my birthday, wedding anniversary, and other celebrated occasions with handwritten, heartfelt notes. They were as long as two sides of the card. During the second half of the marriage, I tried to hold on long enough to receive a card that I hoped would make a deposit in my emotional bank, when in great disappointment, they became the standard Hallmark card with a verbal explanation: "I didn't have time to write anything." It felt like the air had evaporated out of my lungs. I hid the fact that I felt as though I couldn't breathe.

Marriage counseling we attended was an exercise in futility. We stayed in the marriage long after any emotional intimacy was left. It's a lonely place. Still, there is a lot of courage in making a decision to leave what you know and step into the unknown. I am grateful Cab was brave enough to say the words out loud. Or, actually, in my case, send me an email. There it was in my inbox, no surprise however. After a public display of disrespect at dinner with friends over something I said, I was done. Here is how the scene played out:

I was given a voice to participate in the planning of a Christmas party at our new home. Cab's partner had made it clear to me he wanted to stay within a certain budget and the alcohol to be served. Cab started describing the plans for the Christmas party in grandiose description including alcohol that wasn't being served. I made the mistake of correcting him. I realize I may have cut him down in front of our friends. He said, "Fuck you. We don't care about your ideas." I guess that ultimately summed up what I had been feeling all the time. I had just not heard it spoken aloud. I lost all hope of ever returning to the relationship. This was my moment of truth. And so the email concluded: "I give up." I gave up too. Ultimately, this would be the last way we could love each other—enough to say "good-bye."

FUTURE BLENDING OPTIONS

"Men are like wine—some turn to vinegar, but the best improve with age."

Pope John XXIII

The lesson learned here: Life really is too short to drink bad wine. Don't settle. You have to know when to spit it out and dump the bottle. Taste however is subjective—different grapes for different palates. If you pair two compatible grape varietals together, you will have a better chance for a more drinkable experience.

First, you need to identify the varietal you are at your core and the wine experience you deliver. If you're a woman with a strong backbone, you might identify yourself with full-bodied reds. Are you elegant? If so, look for a wine with subtle flavors that are in balance. If expressive, you're a wine that is clear on what you want and project it in your bouquet and flavor. If you're a masculine wine you might smell and taste a bit like woods and mushrooms. Not to worry, it's a good thing. If you're a musky wine you are pleasing to the nose, earthly, masculine, and delicious. An "Oaky" wine does not mean you are from Oklahoma. Oak imparts subtle characteristics on wine, neither feminine nor masculine such as vanilla, spices, and creamy body with an essence of smoky finish. Who doesn't want a creamy body?

Some of the best grape marriages are found in Australia's classic wine blends of Cabernet Sauvignon and Shiraz. Blending Merlot with Cabernet Sauvignon can deliver a richer flavor and smooth out the tannic backbone of the

Cabernet Sauvignon. These marriages seem to stand the test of time—complimentary, and perfectly paired to satisfy your taste for stability. The sex might not be that spicy but they make up for it with consistency. You won't complain you never get any.

If you're a woman looking for a solid relationship, I'd blend with a Cabernet Sauvignon or Zinfandel. Both have complex characteristics and maintain their masculinity with a hint of cigar boxes, and mature with a sweet yet spicy finish. They are intelligent and stimulating, and if stored properly, they will arouse you with their intoxicating aroma that contributes to this unparalleled experience. If they get a bit sassy with bold brash and audacious flavors, just send them to their rooms without any dinner. That'll teach them to exhibit those behaviors.

If you feel like a gamble, try blending with a Pinot Noir—it will either be very good or very bad—there is rarely anything in between. They can be a bit "tight" as well. You will be lucky if they open up enough to reveal themselves to you in your timing. But you will be seduced initially by the silky texture. They have the potential to be very polished and charming with a smooth mouthfeel. A little too volatile for my taste, but could be good for dating, but watch out for their fickle nature. They may love you and leave you.

If you're looking for an Italian to love, and instant gratification, try Sangiovese—which can be drank while still young. A bit one-dimensional but earthy, and they like to be paired. They have a masculine bouquet; they might underestimate their allure which ads to their charm. They are, however, confident in that they never doubt what they are best at. Take a few guesses as to what.

Ask yourself—what kind of grape varietal are you? What type do you pair best with and what type of experience are you looking for? Drink only what gives you joy, delights your palate, and has a nice finish. There is a range of possibilities.

I'm not much of a fan of whites, but I'm open to exploring them further. I feel you need to have some skin in the game to increase your chances for success. In marriage, you get to choose only one. In wine, you get to drink around as much as you want, but be careful not to catch any sediments along the way. Use a condom. And remember, one size does not fit all, in this case.

You'll know the minute it hits your palate, but don't be too quick to judge. You've got to swirl it around for a bit in your mouth before swallowing. Focus on the texture. Is it smooth, creamy, and balanced, or coarse? You may want to, in this case, concern yourself with length, ladies, as this refers to the length of time the wine lingers in your mouth—the longer the better.

Watch out for a hollow experience, which is any wine that has a beginning and a finish, but not much to offer in the middle. Sometimes the initial perception can change the longer you spend time with it. Make sure the experience is consistent before you buy the case. Store it properly and hope it doesn't become corked.

FINDING COURAGE FOR THE JOURNEY

"Courage is fueled by the motivation to take the first step into the unknown."

Cheryl Nielsen

I've often been asked by others contemplating divorce where the courage came from to leave everything I had known. I define courage as the action one takes to step into the unknown fueled by an underlying motivation. In my case, the power to fuel courage was my desire for a better life. Where are you getting your courage? What motivates you to step into this journey?

A dear friend of mine, Debra Oakland, speaks "courage" better than anyone I know in her blog: Living in Courage Online (www.livingincourageonline.com).

This is what she writes:

We're incredibly powerful beings, and yet, as Sting sings, "how fragile we are." There's a bridge between being broken and living in power. We get to choose which side of the bridge to be on. It takes courage to believe in ourselves, to be our true authentic selves, never apologizing for who we are. If we can create a spiritual space inside ourselves, a place where we can overcome life's biggest challenges, we'll truly live in courage. By navigating the bumps in the road wisely, joy becomes a very good travel partner. I truly believe this. We are fragile, powerful, courageous beings experiencing and expressing ourselves in a multitude of ways.

Courage comes in many forms. I like to think of the everyday hero, like you and me. By making wise choices throughout the day, being the best 'you' is courageous, because you are making a conscious choice for good. Sometimes challenges are put in our pathway, not to discourage us, but to call up the qualities of courage that are required, to find the opportunity in the challenge. How you handle these challenges, and the choices you make, determine how smooth or rough the experience will be. It takes courage to be harmless to yourself and others, to ask the question "Is the choice I am making in this moment for the highest and greatest good for myself and for all?" Life expresses out from us according to what is going on inside. Every cell of our body emanates what we are thinking, feeling and acting upon. You may be able to hide things from other people, but never from yourself. We all need 'purpose and direction.' Being true to you should be the first order of business, and that my friend takes great courage. You can grow and be strengthened by challenges. It is a choice, which can create a grand bridge to your joy.

In one of her quotes, Debra says: "Courage is required, down to the very fiber of our existence. Use your will, desire, and persistence to develop the qualities you need to materialize your dreams, whether they are mental, physical, or spiritual." You are more powerful than you realize. We all are. Step up to yourself, for yourself. Find your point of power and connect to it like your life depends upon it, and make courage your constant travel partner."

GRIEF IS THE EMOTIONAL CONTRACT OF DIVORCE

"Sorrow can be alleviated by good sleep, a bath and a glass of good wine."

St. Thomas Aquinas

I thought when I realized intellectually that divorce was the answer, and accepted it at that level, I would escape the emotional pain in the form of grief—as though my intellect could override and control my emotions and I could spare myself the pain. If marriage were only a business contract and not a matter of the heart, perhaps this would have worked. But, ironically, after being emotionally shutdown and unable to feel, I fell into an emotional turmoil for which there was no escaping. Grief overwhelmed me with feelings of sadness, despair, loneliness, and depression.

I tried to find a way out of the pain through distraction, but the grief contract I made with myself was binding. Escaping to a movie or reading a book offered temporary relief. Crying seemed to relieve some of the discomfort I was feeling. I didn't think the grief would be as bad as it was, but whom was I kidding, grief was part of the deal. It came with the territory. I had to realize it was a door I had to go through to complete the healing process. If I tried to deny myself this process, I ran the risk of unresolved issues surfacing again in the future. I had to deal with the loss to have the opportunity to be truly healed. So, I let myself feel. I needed to accept the divorce and mourn the loss on all levels marriage bonded me in—legally, financially, emotionally, spiritually, and physically. I recommend you unpack your emotional baggage while you can. The only bags you want packed here are your soon-to-be ex-wines.

I did not fully anticipate the challenges grief imposed. Transitional decisions were a whole 'nother story. I had lived with the loss of the relationship at many levels while still married. The emotional intimacy was gone, no spiritual connection, and not much going on physically either. Didn't I get a head start in the grieving process? I guess I was kept emotionally alive by the pretend marriage. The one I had on paper accounted for mere "paper loss." Once I pulled the plug, I realized the layers of loss inherent in divorce. Cab was only one layer. I tried to hold on to layers of my life, but as time moved on, I learned that letting go of the old opened the gateway to receiving the new.

At times, it was difficult for me to know precisely what the grief was tied to. Grief became a hodge-podge of emotional soup with loss ingredients such as my ex-wine, friends, house, car, finances, and dreams to name a few. This soup was perfectly spiced with feelings of humiliation, failure, and betrayal—Yum! On closer examination, I couldn't decide if it was a recipe for disaster or health food. Nutrient rich grief is just the nourishment my soul needed to heal. I later came to understand that what I was feeling through the grieving stages of divorce were just that—stages. They did pass. You need to keep in mind that everyone experiences grief differently and for different reasons—your timing to move from one stage to the next will be uniquely yours. Some of the stages most people feel in divorce are:

SHOCK: That point in time when you realize you are getting a divorce. You may feel a paralyzing numbness as though you are a deer caught in headlights—like the time I was at Costco and found a 2001 Beringer Cabernet Sauvignon. I stood frozen—with my eyes wide open. I wasn't sure if I should grab what I could with both hands or take the chance to go get one of those rolling carts, so I could buy all of it before anyone else noticed. The amazing price for it was even more shocking. You may find yourself waking up and having an oh-crap-not-this-life-still morning. That state doesn't rest. It's there to remind you every day. Trust me; this too shall pass.

DENIAL: You've gone through shock, now what? Shock turns to disbelief. I found myself vacillating between reality and denial. Some days, I woke up to believe that it wasn't really happening. I wasn't getting divorced. We would change our minds soon, I thought, or wake up from this bad dream. Imagine if I had given you a bottle of that 2001 Beringer Cabernet Sauvignon and you waited for just the right occasion to open the bottle—perhaps now might be a good time. You cut the seal; you pierce the cork, turn, and pull it from the bottle. You're happy for this moment. Your glass is ready. You pour the first taste. The color is magnificent. You swirl the glass, and in great anticipation, you put your lips to the glass and it's...it's... it's corked! No, can't be, it must be the coffee you just drank, you think to yourself. It's not really corked—denial. You take another sip and another—but still you deny that it's gone bad. You recognize this. This tastes familiar. And that's what happens in divorce too. Divorce is nothing but discovering that your nice bottle of wine has corked. It's time to move on. You'll eventually land the right bottle. Costco might be a good place to start.

ANGER: Anger can manifest itself in many forms. It could be the anger you have toward your ex-wine. It could be something he or she did. Or, it could be anger you have with yourself for the same reasons. You might feel anger toward other people and factors beyond your control. I felt angry because I perceived that Cab moved on very quickly, because he started dating what seemed like right away. I felt betrayed. I wanted more communication from him through the process. There are days when I would look for confrontation. All you need is a reason to take your anger out on someone else during this stage. For me, I would like to personally apologize to the collection companies; they got the majority of my anger—sorry about that, whoever you are.

BARGAINING: At this stage, you might make one last attempt to salvage your marriage by presenting an argument as to why you should stay together, or put further effort into fixing it. The thought did enter my mind. I may have even spoken a reason or two out loud. We had been together for a lot of years. I didn't like to fail. When I had thoughts like this; however, I buried them as deep as I could and told myself to be strong. I believed in my heart that divorce was the right answer. I kept walking toward divorce even if my mind wasn't always with me. Bargaining won't work. If you drink a bottle of corked wine, you can try to pretend it isn't bad. You might even find a way to tolerate the taste. But you must understand you can't reverse what made it bad in the first place. You might be able to make sangria out of it and disguise it under some sweet fruit. Maybe you could introduce another round of malolactic fermentation as a kind of secondary fermentation process and change the bad acid into good acid. This might reduce the acidity and at least give it some additional complexity. Chances are it'll make you sick in the end. When you're corked, you're corked!

GUILT: In hindsight, you might get caught up in the "should've, would've, could've." You might feel guilt for doing or not doing something. Remember, the choices we made then, if we gave it our all, were what we had to work with. I used to beat myself up for not being a bigger person to forgive things that hurt me, or to love my ex-wine unconditionally. I couldn't seem to bring all of me to the table, no matter how much I wanted to. I never cheated on him by blending with any other wine, so I didn't carry this guilt. I did carry the guilt for not being the wine I wanted to be. The one to make the first step to forgive things said or done that hurt me. Instead, the hurts seem to store up inside my wine bottle with the cork on tightly. He can't get in and I can't get out. I thought if I became vulnerable, I would not survive the next sarcastic remark or disappointment. I was afraid my bottle was about to crack and I was going to come spilling out into a puddle on the floor. Neither one of us was willing to make the first move to give the other what we needed. It became a power struggle. If you recall the bottle of corked Beringer I gave you, I feel a little guilty about that because I bought the whole case before I made sure it was a consistent experience and I set you up to fail. So, again, my apology!

DEPRESSION: If you feel fatigued, have an inability to sleep, and feel hopeless and full of despair, you are suffering from depression—the darkest stage of grief. You might want to be evaluated by a mental healthcare professional. You don't want to be here long. Depression would sneak up on me. I'd be going along seemingly fine, working in my business, focused, when all of a sudden; I would fall into what I refer to as the "dark hole": a place full of despair and a lack of hope. It would come out of nowhere like someone switched off the light. The journey was heavy at times, and disappointments would knock the wine out of my hand. Going through a divorce is a tumultuous journey, and you can't always predict the tannins in the process. But one thing is for sure, you can anticipate there will be less-than-smooth times and try to remember there will be good wine in the future—everything will work out in the end. I know it's difficult to believe right now. At this stage, it is good to limit alcohol consumption. There is a time and place for everything.

Alcohol can increase your depressed state. If you become intoxicated, it could lead to episodes in which you "drunk dial" people. This is a pop-culture term describing an instance in which an intoxicated individual places phone calls he or she would not likely make if sober. I drunk dialed friends once and said way more than I ever would have if I weren't drinking. The information gets put out and you can't take it back. Cell phone companies are starting to take notice of this and offer blocking services to help people from falling into this behavior. In Australia, Virgin Mobile offers the ability to let customers block outgoing calls to certain numbers during late-night hours. LG introduced a cell phone in Korea with a built-in breathalyzer. Check with your service provider. You don't want to find yourself calling or texting your ex-wine: "Please take me back. No one tastes as good as you." No wine for me in this stage. Imagine feeling betrayed by a bottle of Cabernet Sauvignon—well then again, I guess I can.

ACCEPTANCE: When you finally get to a point where you accept what is and are willing to work toward the future, you are coming to a stage of acceptance. That's not to say it is a permanent stage. In the grieving process, it is one step forward, two steps back, and so on. As time moves on, you will settle into a more permanent stage of acceptance. Once you get to this stage for any amount of time, you may start to feel as I did: that it's time to work through the divorce process and get on with a new life, and ultimately, with a new wine. I started to believe there was a life to be had after divorce. I accepted where I was and became excited for the future.

It's important to be mindful of where you are in the stages of grief. You might want to keep a journal and write down your feelings. You can reflect on your entries, see patterns, and see the progress you are making. You might find you still have plenty of things to be grateful for; focus on those as well. It is critical to allow yourself to grieve. Mourning your losses will help un-blend you from all the marriage bonds—legal, financial, emotional, and spiritual. Let's not forget physical bond.

I didn't find a loophole to get out of the emotional contract of divorce. Grief, in hindsight, was just what I needed to heal. It forced me to slow down, deal with my feelings, and adapt to dramatic life changes. As I slowed down, it was like all the emotions I had suppressed in the past started surfacing. No longer distracted by the life I was living, I used the solitude I found myself in to bring these emotions to the surface of my awareness, and by doing so, I allowed myself to feel the full impact of the pain in hopes of bringing closure and releasing them. I also used this time to get back in touch with myself and become reacquainted with whom I am and how I plan to live my life moving forward. It launched me into self-discovery.

Divorce is one time in your life when you get to return to your authentic form—stripped of the life that produced you, but able to retain the wisdom of the experience. I came to realize I was re-producing myself. My soul was going through subtle changes like wine does in a barrel, and I was preparing for my release on the other side.

YOU'RE GOING BACK IN THE BARREL

"People of balance age as gracefully as wines of balance."

John Jordan, Jordan Vineyard & Winery

Divorce offers an opportunity to go back into the barrel and become the wine you want to be—a kind of "barrel refinement process." You are the winemaker. Hop in—it's a good place to hide out, safe and warm. The wood will protect your fragile being and hold you together. You get to re-produce yourself in here—make the most of this time communing with yourself. You're going to spend some time drinking your own wine—spitting out what you don't like along the way, and deciding what you swallow. You have to be courageous and learn to live by faith, as it can be dark in the barrel—but there is wine, and that is a good thing.

The length of time wine spends in the barrel is dependent upon the varietal and style of wine the winemaker chooses to make. Pinot Noir may spend less than a year in a barrel, while a Cabernet Sauvignon to blow your palate may spend up to two years. Your length of time in the barrel will be uniquely yours and according to the wine you want to become. Take your time, you are building character, it can't be rushed if you want to mature to perfection.

Wine as it rests in a barrel goes through subtle chemical changes, resulting in greater complexity and character. It also softens the harsh tannins. The barrel imparts the character of the wood into the wine and delivers distinctive flavors and sophistication. The time you rest in the barrel will have a profound effect upon the wine you become. Tears of sorrow will enhance the flavor. Your personal growth, reflection, and self-discovery will deliver character. The tannins of your backbone will become smooth with perspective, compassion, and humility. Your character may change—even your body.

My time in the barrel delivered a spicier and more complex version of me on the other side— no longer a flat, one-dimensional wine that rarely came out to play. This wine likes to open up and have fun. The experience awakened a higher spiritual awareness as a result of having only faith and a barrel to carry me through the darkness of loss and grief. I got back in touch with the varietal of my core and realigned with my authentic self. I didn't need a label. I've learned how to be happy with what's inside. It became easier to let go of the labels of the past, while I embraced the wine I became with a purpose for the future—a wine to be shared, appreciated, and enjoyed for those willing to drink. I was transformed; you will be too. After you take this journey, you will see how.

You might try to escape the barrel with thoughts that you are a good wine already. Why go back into the barrel? If you try to resist, you will deny your soul a chance to use this experience to re-produce you; therefore, you are at risk of becoming bitter and undrinkable. If you don't go into the barrel willingly now, you might get another opportunity in the future because your soul could be asking for this experience. The divorce may be a symptom of something buried in you that needs to be identified and healed from, so you can be in alignment with your authentic self and, therefore, able to live your best life. At least it was for me.

Escape the barrel and life may provide another opportunity—another wake-up call. Eventually, you are going in whether you want to or not. Do it now. Opportunity is knocking. Relax; after you are re-produced, you'll like the new wine you become. People will want to drink you up for your richness of flavor—matured to perfection, perhaps with a little pepper around the edges for distinction. The depth of your character will be deeper and more flavorful. You will be smoother on the palate and softer on the finish. You'll enjoy getting back in your bottle with increased confidence and going on the tasting appointments of life. You will deliver an authentic experience because you will have the opportunity to get back into your own skin. It is the skin of the grape that gives wine color. That's why I drink reds over whites—they have more skin in the game. You will too.

When I gave myself over to the barrel refinement process, it was as though everything I was running from—all the demons of the past—were cast into the barrel with me. For all intents and purposes, the barrel was purgatory and I had to decide if I was going to see the light of day, or if I was going to live forever in the dark. Demons don't like light, so you have to spend time with them in the dark on their turf. It's the only way you can see them. You can offer them wine in the barrel; they'll open up more and you can wrestle with them better. In the end, by confronting them, they will lose their power and evaporate into thin air just as alcohol burns off when cooking with it.

It was a dark journey for me, but it was worth it. The time I spent in the barrel refinement process through my divorce was a time of personal reflection, learning, and spiritual growth. A journey I would not have taken otherwise, that changed my perspective, and reconnected me with the real wine I am, not the type of wine that hides under labels. I like the new wine I am. It makes the old me look like a young undrinkable wine. In hindsight, divorce gave me the opportunity of a lifetime.

Have you ever wondered what happens inside a wine barrel? *This video will illustrate:*

Winemaking in action: battonage in clear-top Chardonnay wine barrel

http://www.bit.ly/jordancleartop

Watch Jordan Winery's Cellar Master Patrick Fallon perform battonage (the stirring of the Chardonnay lees) inside a demonstration wine barrel.

29

WINE PROFILING

"Wine is like the incarnation—it is both divine and human."

Paul Tillich

The first step in the barrel refinement process is to decide the wine you want to become. You need to create a wine profile. Think of the most amazing wine you have ever experienced out of a bottle. Perhaps you won't recall the name, but the essence of it. Ask yourself what made it so special. What are some of the characteristics of this wine that appealed to you? Perhaps you can draw on this experience to capture the characteristics you desire in yourself. This will be your winemaking formula for how you want to re-produce yourself and ultimately be released on the other side.

Next, choose a wine to represent you that has the characteristics you desire in yourself and delivers this experience. This will create a wine vision for your character refinement. Taste is subjective. If you like it, chances are someone else will too. Select a few wines at your local wine shop and identify some key components. Describe the wine with tasting notes and pull out the notes that you would like in your character. Here is my example:

The characteristics I have chosen for my character refinement are: mature with a seductive bouquet, intelligent, bold, complex, edgy, but elegant, with a creamy finish.

The bottle of wine I have chosen for my wine vision to represent me is a 2001 Jordan, Cabernet Sauvignon.

What are the characteristics you have chosen for your character refinement?

The bottle of wine you have chosen to represent you is:

WOULD THE REAL WINE PLEASE STAND UP?

"Good wine is a good familiar creature if it be well used."

William Shakespeare (1564-1616)
Othello, II. iii. (315)

In the early stages of divorce, I recall feeling naked and exposed, as though the label that clothed me was torn from my bottle and I became a "shiner," basically an unlabeled wine. The label I had went through the paper shredder and I found myself constantly trying to tape it back together to define the wine I once felt I was—the all-encompassing complex and proud wine that was defined by the label I had worn each day as a wife, a business owner, the gracious hostess, a vineyard owner, and the list goes on.

These labels had an ego value attached to them that defined my worth to not only me, but to the outside world. For years, I felt I knew whom I was and what I was supposed to do when I woke up in the morning. It's easy to get caught up in life with the labels that we play as a wife, or the identity we give ourselves, and society gives us as a result of our professions, social status, money, etc. With each label comes a role to play that includes a certain set of expectations from ourselves, others, and society.

When I lost the labels and identity of being blended, wealthy, and successful in my business to name a few, to catastrophic loss, I had no labels to hide behind. I had very little identity to hold on to that defined me or to hold up to the world and say, "This is me. This is who I am." I had no choice other than to find a way to value myself without the labels that once did. It was scary. I worked most of my life striving to earn respect, love, and security outwardly from others and through material things. Little did I know that the only respect, love, and security that will ever last is the respect, love, and security that lies within me on the inside of the bottle and that I have for my wine-self. Not just any wine-self, but for my authentic wine-self.

I can't put limitations on loving only the parts of me that I like and ignoring the parts that I don't. This conditional love is not real love. Accepting all parts of me and making allowances for my shortcomings is part of being human-wine and necessary to fully embrace my authentic wine-self. When I was stripped of my labels and the roles that defined me, I was given the chance of a lifetime to re-produce that inner being that was overlooked and put aside.

It takes a lot of energy to deny ourselves. Can you think of all the times in your life you had a desire for something, or a need, and you dismissed it as selfish, irresponsible, inappropriate, or impossible? Labels can be limiting. Marriage can be stifling if we lose ourselves in the relationship and role-play to our blended wine's desires while denying our own. If I had been more in-touch with my authentic wine-self and less caught up in the labels I was playing, perhaps I would not have suffered such an identity crisis. Perhaps if I loved myself, I could have allowed more emotional deposits to enter instead of dismissing them because they could not penetrate my layer of unworthiness. My life would have changed, but I still would have had me independent of labels and intact.

I woke up, however, and found out that I was not in-touch with my authentic wine-self. I had lost me a long time ago—too long ago to remember. I was running on empty. Maybe it was at age five. I remember being consciously aware that if I needed or asked for something, I would most likely not be heard or get it. I started suppressing my needs. I learned how to go unnoticed. I felt like I was in a movie most of the time, watching life from the outside while being detached on the inside. I thought others were selfish that were too into themselves by prioritizing their wants and desires first over anything else.

Ever notice how many relationships are conditional? A life lived within an all-too-common phrase—"you uncork my bottle and I'll uncork yours." I struggled with feeling anyone could be happy to spend time with me just to drink my wine as a main course without something paired. Maybe I would take them to lunch or bring them a little gift—"a little food with your wine?" I never felt good enough to stand alone. At least they received something. Not a complete waste of their time. No wonder I was so emotionally bankrupted.

I'm not sure if the divorce was from Cab or with my authentic wine-self when I made the decision to deny meeting my own needs and living authentically. This authentic-self embraces who we really are under all those labels. She's like my long lost friend. Our constant companions are ourselves. We have to like spending time drinking our own wine. Take the time to become acquainted again—the taste will be comforting to your soul.

Your authentic self will not only be your inner child-wine but the adult-wine that has been refined and matured through your life experience and barrel refinement process. It's like knowing what you know now, but applying it to what you didn't know then. If you had talents when you were younger that were not fully developed, isn't it going to be easier to bring those out now?

Feelings and actions can be in constant contradiction. I think of all the people who go to church, thinking they can feel good about themselves for a while when they are just there going through the motions of acting and behaving less than their authentic selves. This type of hypocrisy exists in everyday life when we do things just because we think we should, or to reinforce some image of our false label. This kind of phony behavior projects something other than what we really are and can be an energy drain on our emotional reserves.

Any time we spend time giving energy that is not in line with our authentic wine-self we are not having a healthy exchange of emotional currency. Spend more than your deposits and you are emotionally bankrupt. Being truly authentic will allow us to experience joy and happiness in our lives. We need not prove anything to any other wine. We have value in the form of our unique taste and characteristics that, at the very least, if authentic, will project honesty—a characteristic that delivers a consistent and trustworthy experience when others drink us.

By removing the labels of ego value and embracing my authentic wine-self, I no longer judged my reality by my own limiting beliefs. It altered my perception of life in a profound way. I adopted more gray areas in my belief system. Not such a black-and-white version of perfection I strived for before. As a result, I became more tolerant, compassionate and understanding of myself and others and I was able to relate to and find joy, nourishment, and pleasure in being around people who were not afraid to be themselves. It felt good and refreshing to "let it all hang out," the good, the bad, and the ugly. I finally joined the human-wine race.

EMBRACE YOUR AUTHENTIC WINE-SELF

How do we go about reconnecting with that authentic wine-self that may have been lost or denied? Or, how can we live the most authentic wine life? I suggest making a list of the ways you can practice being true to yourself. Make sure to shed the old labels that are not in line with your authentic wine-self. Once you adapt ways to honor your authentic wine-self and incorporate them into your wine-life, you will be living authentically.

For example, here is my list of ways I will practice being authentic:

1. STOP ACTING: Be genuine. Say what I really feel, tactfully.
2. LEARN TO SAY "NO": Use my energy for my higher purpose, not other wines' agendas.
3. DON'T VOLUNTEER TO DO MORE THAN WHAT IS REQUIRED ALL THE TIME: Over achieving can draw from the energy for tomorrow!
4. LISTEN TO MY BODY AND REST WHEN NECESSARY: My health comes first over recognition for a job well done.
5. SCHEDULE ME TIME FIRST: I will prioritize maintaining my emotional, physical, and spiritual health before anything else.
6. LISTEN TO MY INTERNAL INTUITION: Recognize red flags. Maintain a journal to watch for the signs and trust my intuition.
7. WAIT PATIENTLY FOR THE RIGHT ANSWERS TO COME: Use natural timing to make decisions, not my will.

8. RECOGNIZE THAT PARTS OF ME I DON'T LIKE ARE PARTS OF ME AS WELL: No wine is perfect; although, some comes pretty close!

9. RECREATE AND REJUVENATE WITHOUT GUILT: I require time off, so I don't become "corked." Vacations are mandatory, even massages!

10. USE MY TALENTS: Don't feel insecure. Believe in myself and that I was created by the master winemaker—GOD!

11. RECOGNIZE MY UNIQUE ABILITIES: Embrace my abilities—they can be used for my divine purpose for which I was designed.

12. BE WILLING TO RECEIVE FROM OTHERS: Ask for help when I need it, and realize others need to fulfill their purpose too.

13. GRACIOUSLY ACCEPT A COMPLIMENT AND BELIEVE IT'S MEANT: Don't block emotional deposits; allow them to fill me up.

14. WHEN LIFE GIVES ME WATER, TURN IT INTO WINE: Look for opportunities when circumstances seem dismal.

15. RECOGNIZE THE WISDOM OF THE EXPERIENCE AND USE IT: Everything in life is meant to teach; look for the lesson. I don't want to take a course over again if I don't have to.

16. PLAY LIKE A KID SOMETIMES: I'm never too old to play with wonder.

17. ALLOW MYSELF TO RELAX: I'm not being lazy if I want to sit on the beach and read a book—quiet time is what I need to align with my higher-self and to be guided internally.

18. ALLOW MYSELF TO FEEL: It's okay to admit when I am sad, scared, hurt, or angry for this is how I know I am alive and able to feel.

19. EXERCISE FOR FITNESS AND BODY CONFIDENCE: Design a workout plan that is doable and gives me the results I am looking for, and make it part of everyday living.

20. TRY NEW THINGS: Maybe I'll take an art class. Even if I can't draw—doesn't mean I can't paint!

21. BE OPEN MINDED: Expand my palate—I might be surprised what I acquire a taste for.

22. RECOGNIZE THE JOY IN THE MOMENT: Take in the sunrise in the morning, or capture a walk in the rain.

23. BE CONTENT WITH LESS: Material things own me; I don't own them—less is more.
24. APPRECIATE THE GOOD IN OTHERS: Perhaps I won't like everything about the wine, perhaps that white will be good only when I am eating fish.
25. LET GO OF LIMITING BELIEFS: Don't box myself in around my label; I can revise it and grow to new levels of understanding, consciousness, and spirituality at any time. I am never "done."
26. BE HONEST WITH MYSELF: A major ingredient to an authentic relationship with myself. If I can't master this one, it will be difficult to get anyone else to drink my wine.
27. RID MYSELF OF TOXIC RELATIONSHIPS: If I sense a relationship is not serving my higher purpose and it drains me of my energy—I will rid myself of it, it is acidic and potentially a carrier of an emotional virus.
28. REMEMBER THAT AGE IS ONLY A NUMBER: It is never too late to turn back the clock and improve my health and vitality. I am never too old for blending!
29. RECOGNIZE THE MIRACLES IN LIFE: Take note in a journal and watch how many there are. It will surprise me.
30. RECOGNIZE MY NEEDS: This is a big one for me. I've prided myself on not having any. But I can't get my needs met by drinking my own wine—I need to blend, and communicate with other wine to better understand who I am and to evolve.
31. ALLOW LOVE TO ENTER MY LIFE: Feel worthy and appreciate myself for who I am. A unique and special wine.
32. USE EACH EXPERIENCE TO TEACH ME SOMETHING: Take in the wisdom, reflect, and learn the lesson.
33. EXERCISE GOOD BOUNDARIES WITH OTHERS: Don't let them take more from me than feels comfortable. Watch for a healthy exchange of energy.
34. DON'T TAKE WINE AT ITS LABEL: Look inside the bottle and give it a try first.
35. REFLECT ON GRATITUDE: Appreciate each moment and everything and everyone I have in my life to be grateful for.

Your turn:

Make a list of the ways that you can practice being authentic:

AUTHENTIC WINE LIFE STATEMENT

"To take wine into your mouth is to savor a droplet of the river of human history."

Clifton Fadiman, N. Y. Times, 8 Mar '87

As of now, you have created a wine profile of the characteristics you would like in yourself. You have also identified ways of being authentic and living an authentic life. This information can be blended together to create a wine-life statement of how you want to live your life after divorce.

Here is my authentic wine life statement:

To live life with an authentic label and appreciate me for the wine I am and the unique characteristics I deliver. To embrace life with openness, with the courage to put myself out there and risk being spit out. To never settle for less than what I deserve. To love myself and balance my physical, emotional, and spiritual needs, so I don't become corked. To always remember that taste is subjective; there really is no bad wine. To always look at life through wine-colored glasses.

Now create your authentic wine life statement:

WINE LIFE VISION BOARD

"If you see in your wine the reflection of a person not in your range of vision, don't drink it."

Chinese Proverb

You've got to have dreams and goals to build a plan around them. This plan is the root stock that will be planted into your optimally cultivated soil. It is the plan your professionals will use to assist you in preparing the soil—so you can grow your new life. If you aspire to travel four months out of the year, it might be a good idea if your financial planner knows, so he can design a financial plan to support your dream.

My authentic wine-self has many desires too. In a workshop, I had the opportunity to create a vision board—a collage of images (mainly pictures cut from magazines and publications) that represent the vision I have for how I want to rebuild my life with my heart's desires. The images are from my heart and soul and not from my head. They represent what I really want without regard to limiting beliefs, notions of what I think I should do, or practicality. It's purely right-brained and a creative download of tapping into my underlying passions and desires. I turn to my vision board as a constant source of inspiration and barometer of staying on track with my dreams and goals. Purchase a poster board at an office supply store, a glue pen, and a pair of scissors. Cut out images from magazines that represent your dreams and goals or use your artistic talents to draw. Some reflections of my goals:

1. Travel – a picture of Italy's countryside
2. Publish a book – a drawing of a book with my name on the cover
3. New Friends – a scene of a dinner party with food and wine
4. House – a picture of a small bungalow beach property
5. Body Confidence – a picture of a bikini
6. Love – a couple embracing
7. Financial stability – a drawing of money
8. Good Health – a picture of a marathon runner
9. Spiritual Awareness – a picture of the ocean and sunset

To organize your images electronically, visit www.pinterest. com. This is the ultimate online pin-board to organize and share things you love that would work well to create your wine-life vision board.

Now that we have an idea of the wine we want to become, how we want to be drank, and our vision for the future, we can forge ahead with the details of un-blending financially from our spouse.

PREPARE YOUR SOIL

"One of life's gifts is that each of us, no matter how tired and downtrodden, finds reasons for thankfulness: for the crops carried in from the fields and the grapes from the vineyard."

J. Robert Moskin

The time you are in the barrel having the opportunity to re-produce yourself, you will most likely still be grieving which will render your decision-making capacity compromised. You might start your transitional divorce process in any stage of grief—even before acceptance. The emotions that accompany each stage will make you less than objective in making decisions. These decisions may impact the rest of your life.

If your judgment is clouded, it might be a good idea to delay signing any paperwork or making any permanent decisions. You don't want to give your ex-wine all the wine just because you are feeling guilty about something. You'll need some of that wine to drink too. It is absolutely necessary to rely on industry professionals to guide you through the process. How you transition your life will determine the stability and growth of your future. Before you sign that last document to lock in your divorce agreement, you, hopefully, have done the right amount of research and planning to insure your success for the future.

I liken it to starting a vineyard. I had the privilege to do this in my life. There is a certain amount of research that must be done up front before you plant vines—if you want to ensure they will grow properly in the future. There are no shortcuts.

Chances are you will need to consult with a number of industry professionals.

First off, the soil needs to be tested. Different grape varietals require different soil that delivers unique compositions that varietal must have to survive and thrive. Plant in soil that is not conducive or properly cultivated for that varietal and you've wasted your efforts and set yourself up for failure in the future.

You also need a proper support system for the vines in the form of trellising, so the plants can be guided to maturity. They are simply not left on their own to grow aimlessly in the soil. They have an end product in mind—wine. They want to grow up to produce a grape with a purpose—to contribute to the lives of those who appreciate them for what they ultimately become—the delicious essence of that bottle of wine enjoyed by those who drink it.

The vines need to be nourished. They need to be watered properly. Water too much and the roots could develop fungus, too little and the roots don't develop. A drip system of consistent and timely water optimizes the chances for success. A boost of fertilizer provides the vines the nutrients they need to grow.

The point is: you can't build a new life on bad soil. You have to decide first off what kind of varietal you want to be and the finished product you want to become. Do you want to be smooth and refined, matured to perfection on the other side, or do you want to die on the vine? To optimize your chances for success, you need to get a team of professionals: financial professionals, wellness professionals, and spiritual professionals to provide the proper guidance and support.

Just like a vineyard has a vineyard support system, we as humans in the form of wine going through divorce need a divorce support system. Both systems support the foundation to grow on—the rest is up to Mother Nature and us as individuals. It's a time to ask for help. You can't be expected to make clear decisions even if you are an industry professional on a particular subject matter. Get out of your own way and let God and others carry this burden right now. You will have enough emotional baggage to carry for a while.

Prepare your soil and you will reap a harvest in the future. This video captures the harvest of Cabernet Sauvignon grapes in the heart of Alexander Valley.

Harvesting hillside vineyards of Alexander Valley Cabernet Sauvignon

http://www.bit.ly/jordanhillside

Jordan Vineyard & Winery describes it as follows:

Scenes from the morning harvest of hillside Cabernet Sauvignon grapes grown in the heart of Alexander Valley. One of our top family growers and his dog, Abby, make a few appearances. All of the grapes harvested for Jordan Cabernet Sauvignon are picked when our Winemaker Rob Davis believes the flavors are ideal for making a beautifully balanced, elegant, silky wine.

PICKING YOUR DIVORCE SUPPORT SYSTEM

In preparation of divorce, start picking the components of your divorce support system, so they are in place, ready to support your financial, physical, emotional, and spiritual needs. Your divorce support system will be uniquely yours to fit your specific needs and goals. Be reluctant to work with family or friends who can be less than objective and emotionally involved, not to mention they most likely do not have the appropriate level of expertise to guide you properly. Consider some of the following for your divorce support system:

DIVORCE COACH

1. Meritage Divorce Coach, CDC Certified Divorce Coach, Collaborative Divorce Coach

FINANCIAL/LEGAL

1. Divorce Attorney, Mediator, or Collaborative Divorce Specialist
2. Certified Financial Planner and/or Certified Divorce Financial Analyst
3. Certified Public Accountant
4. Forensic Accountant
5. Bankruptcy Attorney
6. Estate Planning Attorney
7. Real Estate Broker
8. Real Estate Appraiser
9. Banker

MERITAGE DIVORCE

10. Insurance Agents – Health, Life, Disability, Business
11. Credit Counselors
12. Business Appraisers
13. Bookkeeper
14. Private Investigators
15. Administrative Services – errands, etc.

PHYSICAL

1. Medical Doctor
2. Wellness Doctor
3. Personal Trainer/Gym/Exercise Program/Yoga
4. Spa/Massage Therapist
5. Hair Stylist
6. Manicurist
7. Nutritionist
8. Vitamins
9. Good Food & Wine

EMOTIONAL

1. Psychiatrist, Psychologist, Therapist, Counselor
2. Group Therapy
3. Divorce Support Groups
4. Friends & Family
5. Pets
6. Books

SPIRITUAL

1. Religious – Priest, Minister, Rabi, Pastor, or other
2. Metaphysics
3. Intuitive
4. Meditation
5. Nature
6. Hobbies
7. Recreation
8. Passions

Now that you have some idea of what a divorce support system might look like, it's time to pick a core layer of support. As time moves on, you might engage with additional support as needed.

Using the examples above, begin identifying resources that you have and other resources that you need to find. Research professional qualifications carefully, and don't decide on anyone until you know they are the right fit for you.

DISMANTLING FINANCIAL ASSETS

"You have only so many bottles in your life, never drink a bad one."

Len Evans

It took years for Cab and me to acquire our financial assets—several businesses and real estate holdings with complex structures that all needed to be restructured, sold, or dismantled in some manner. A complicated undertaking I refer to as "delicate financial pruning"—one wrong move and I've cut off too much.

I wanted out of the complexity and pressure of managing so many moving parts. I knew it wouldn't happen overnight due to the fact that I needed to be very strategic in my exit strategy, so as not to trigger unwanted financial ramifications—particularly in the form of income taxes. Execution of some of the dismantling would be contingent upon market timing and other factors beyond my immediate control.

Cab and I worked through much of our divorce with a mediator. Our situation was financially complicated and it sometimes felt more exhausting to explain it to someone else. So, I took the lead, digging in and trying to identify all the underlying complexity of our financial situation. I consulted with other financial professionals, but I took the responsibility for designing the plan. I had spreadsheets coming out of my bottle. Taking the lead to identify and direct our marital settlement agreement was a daunting task and rendered me exhausted. In hindsight, I built a plan that ultimately failed. I had not done enough planning with the right professionals and as a result, I had to weather much financial hardship post-divorce that I could have been spared had I got my know-it-all ego out of the way and consulted with more professionals.

Using the vineyard analogy—the plan or marital settlement agreement was the root stock that I planted into the soil. I failed to realize that I did not cultivate the soil properly. There were underlying rocks in the soil that prevented the roots from taking hold. Weeds, as well, choked the vines as they started to grow—these issues were not apparent on the surface using my "eye level" of expertise. I was not in a position to know this; it was out of my line of vision. In short, I didn't know what I didn't know. I had no business taking the lead. The plan failed to account for contingencies. If everything went according to plan, it would be an ideal situation, however there are circumstances that can come up that require contingencies or "what if" scenario back-up plans.

As time moved on post-divorce, I was presented with the flaws of the plan I designed. Being consumed with grief left my critical thinking skills compromised at the time. Even though I was a real estate broker by profession, I could not make objective decisions for myself on my real estate holdings. If representing a client, I would have known better.

One of my mistakes was an emotional decision to take title back to a property before my divorce was final. I thought it would be a good house to start over in once I sold the vineyard estate. The problem was that it was rented out for several years and the underlying tax structure on it had changed from a primary residence to investment property and was no longer subject to tax-free gains when selling it. It was sitting on a tax time bomb. If I sold it or it foreclosed, I would have huge capital gains issues—even if there were no proceeds from the sale—in the form of "paper gains."

The value was upside down and the sale of it—if I could not make it work to live in financially—would be a short-pay to the lender. I could be exposed for collection on the deficient pay-off (as well as my ex-wine who was still on the loan). And, additionally, this cancellation of debt amount would be considered income. Clearly, I just inherited a toxic asset! Not a good plan. I had two choices: make it work, or suffer severe tax consequences if I didn't. If I had to do it over again, I would not have taken title back to the property.

Another huge mistake I made was to liquidate my retirement accounts to pay off credit-card debt. Even though I was able to settle the debt for pennies on the dollar, I exchanged the difference for a tax bill from the IRS and state. I would have been in better shape to owe a bank, not to mention, credit card debt can be discharged or reorganized through bankruptcy law. Taxes are difficult to discharge as there are a number of conditions that must be met.

It's also important to watch your language and structure in your divorce settlement. If you receive income from a property settlement and decide you need to file bankruptcy later, a bankruptcy trustee might look at some of the income you receive as an asset that could be liquidated or sold to pay creditors. You could lose your income stream.

Having a flexible plan that would provide for some of the contingencies or worst-case scenarios was missing. If I had it to do over, I would approach the situation differently.

I would have consulted with an entire team of financial professionals. A good financial team includes the following financial professionals: certified financial planner (CFP) or certified divorce financial analyst (CDFA), certified public accountant (CPA), estate planning attorney, real estate broker, and bankruptcy attorney.

Note that I did not mention a divorce attorney. Unless they are certified, licensed, and/or trained in these other fields, they can't give you expert advice on financial matters, taxes, real estate, or even bankruptcy law. They simply do not have the expertise. Therefore, a divorce attorney should not be the one directing or making recommendations for the disposition of financial assets in the process! Who directs the process? The answer: The certified financial planner (CFP) or certified divorce financial analyst (CDFA)!

A good CFP or CDFA can be considered the soil cultivator of your team of financial professionals. They will be able to see the rocks and weeds in your financial make-up that they can address through proper resourcing, whether that is a certified public accountant (CPA), or other financial professional. A CFP or CDFA will come up with a strategy or list of recommendations after carefully reviewing your financial situation and consulting with the proper professionals.

Having the insight of the ramifications of separating financial assets will help facilitate the agreement you and your spouse make to separate your assets. The process of working with the

CFP or CDFA will provide the best possible financial outcome for your personal situation. You can see a financial planner with your soon-to-be ex-wine or you can go alone. It depends upon the current state of the relationship. If you are on good terms and are working together cooperatively and communicating well, it could work meeting together. If you both are working with separate divorce attorneys, go it alone. Find out what works best for you with the assistance of your financial planner and use this information to direct your settlement negotiations.

This financial planning process will also provide a plan of action for the future to assist you in rebuilding your financial future. That is why it is important to have some idea of what you want your new life to look like. This experience will prove immeasurable and give you lots of peace of mind. The relationship you build will support you well in the future as financial matters change. The financial planner will be an integral player to maximize your financial well-being.

In order to make proper decisions on your financial dismantling and future, you must first make an accurate list of all your financial assets. Once you have this list together, you will be in a position to have an intelligent conversation with a financial planner. You might also see opportunities to use the financial assets you have in more creative ways. Don't start making any decisions right away—seek the advice of this financial expert, and spare yourself the ramifications of costly mistakes that are sometimes impossible to unwind. If you are unsure of all the financial assets and how to identify them because your spouse handled the financial affairs, your tax returns are a good source of information. Identify what you can and take your tax returns with you to meet with the financial planner. Here are some of the areas your divorce financial planner should be able to address or help resource:

- Establishing financial needs and strategies to pay
- Real estate analysis
    Referred to a real estate broker if necessary
- Strategies to minimize taxes
    Referred to a CPA if necessary
- Analysis of settlement scenarios
- Short-term and long-term financial implications of alternative settlement scenarios

- Dividing pension plans
- Continued health coverage
- Making financial sense of proposals
- Cash management and spending plans
- Retirement needs and goal setting
- Social Security estimations and benefits
- Estate planning issues
      Referred to an estate planning attorney if necessary
- Planning for future financial needs
- Planning for retirement
- Planning for college funds

Now that I have identified that the most important role in a divorce is the financial planner, perhaps this will assist in the route you would like to take to initiate the legal process of divorce.

THE LEGAL BUSINESS OF DIVORCE

"Pinot Noir is more than just another varietal; it is seductive and ephemeral and attracts a fiercely independent, opinionated breed."

Lance Cutler, *Wine Business Monthly*

There are a few different paths you can take to initiate the legal process of divorce and to reach a settlement agreement. It's important to establish the path early on because if you or your soon-to-be ex-wine retain an attorney and start the process, it will make it difficult to choose another path. Getting educated first on your options is a must, and agreeing with each other on the path to take before a decision is made independently would be ideal.

The obvious path most take is to retain a divorce attorney. Get your checkbook ready; this is going to be expensive if litigation is involved. Additionally, anything you consult with an attorney about that is outside his or her "highest and best use," you will pay a premium for. These would include conversations not directly related to the legal aspects of divorce. Do you think you might have a need to discuss divorce related issues that are not necessarily legal issues?

Another path you can choose is a cooperative divorce model through a mediator or collaborative divorce team. This model introduces a neutral financial specialist to address financial and tax matters between both parties. The neutrality streamlines the data gathering and can be substantially less expensive than working with an attorney within a litigation model known as "discovery." The use of a neutral financial specialist is relatively new, but a growing trend. With a clear and comprehensive picture of the overall finances and an understanding of each party's realistic needs, the financial specialist can make recommendations that are focused on maximizing the available assets to best meet the needs of each party, rather than trying to get the most for one party without regard for the other.

In this model, the financial specialist must adhere to the ethical standard that prevents her or him from continuing in any client relationship after the divorce that would compromise the neutral position. The standard does not preclude him or her from addressing issues that arise relative to the divorce process that may require follow-up in the future. A new financial planner relationship would need to be retained after the divorce is final. In a collaborative divorce, the spouses seek to reach an agreement with each other without going to court. The final settlement agreement is taken to a judge for a final divorce decree.

There are other paths outside retaining an attorney and litigating, and the cooperative model. You might be able to find other paths, but these two paths are the ones most travelled.

It is important to note that not all financial specialists are alike. The Institute for Divorce Financial Analysts™ offers comprehensive training using a variety of knowledge and skill-building techniques. To acquire the designation, a candidate must successfully pass all exams. Some of the areas the training covers are:

- Personal vs. marital property
- Valuing and dividing property
- Retirement assets and pensions
- Spousal and child support
- Splitting the house
- Tax problems and solutions
- Tax law and financial issues affecting divorce

In the financial planning industry, there are a number of qualified financial planners that are competent to deal with divorce issues outside the (CDFA) certification. Some of which might be certified as a financial planner (CFP).

MAKING WINE OUT OF WATER

"We hear of the conversion of water into wine at the marriage in Cana, as of a miracle. But this conversion is, through the goodness of God, made every day before our eyes. Behold the rain which descends from heaven upon our vineyards, and which incorporates itself with the grapes to be changed into wine; a constant proof that God loves us, and loves to see us happy!"

Benjamin Franklin -*The Posthumous and Other Writings of Benjamin Franklin* (1819)

It became apparent that the property Cab and I had acquired just a year prior to separating could not be sustained financially by either one of us—it would need to be sold. I took ownership of this property and listed it right away while I continued to live in it while marketing it for sale. It was 2008 and the real estate market was taking a beating. It would be difficult to unload a large estate on four acres with a Cabernet vineyard in Orange County. Luxury real estate was not moving. It was nearly impossible to get a lender to finance these higher loan amounts (3.89 million) even if you had a ready and willing buyer. I needed a plan to subsidize it financially until I could find the right buyer—someone who was a wine enthusiast, or liked horses, maybe cars, and had plenty of money!

After listing the property for sale, people would find it online and call me to inquire if they could rent it for vacation, or for a wedding. There seemed to be a demand for a unique property for special events in Orange County. This gave me the idea to convert the property into a venue to be used for weddings and private events.

Orange County is generally very dense living with the exception of a few areas. Trabuco Canyon is one of them. The area off Live Oak Canyon is rural horse country. There are many homes situated on multi-acre lots. Cab and I bought this property while it was under construction and we were vacationing in Tuscany, Italy. It lies nestled in the canyon behind a rod iron gate at the end of a private road. Each time I reached the high point of the road before it descended to the driveway, the property would take my breath away. It looked like a painting of an Italian Villa and countryside.

I spent the first year upgrading it and overseeing the implementation of the six-hundred-vine Cabernet Sauvignon vineyard that surrounded the large estate with the appropriate sloping hillside. The property offered multiple outdoor platforms for large-scale entertaining that included an internal courtyard, large sprawling lawn, and tiered patio large enough for one hundred and fifty chairs, complete with a stage area overlooking the vineyard.The grounds were laced with fragrant lavender plants that fed the senses and the forest backdrop gave way to the most breathtaking views. After a rain, it gifted a fragrant bouquet of woods, grasses, and other earthly delights.

At sunset on any given day, I was overjoyed to see a family of deer grazing along the private drive to the property. I made their acquaintance by pulling over in my car, rolling down the window and saying a few words, hoping they would recognize my voice over time. Their ears twitched and they remained undisturbed, yet curious.

One evening, I was awakened from a deep sleep to hear screeching outside and loud banging noises. I thought I was up againsta home-invasion robbery.I jumped out of bed and grabbed an enormous flashlight and headed to the deck adjacent the master bedroom. I shinned the light onto the grounds and found a real buck on top of the bronze doe deer, purchased at an auction, trying to mate. As the flashlight caught his eyes, I noticed he seemed a little frustrated.He must have thought, "Gee, what am I doing wrong here?" Even more interesting is that the buck jumped off and let another one have a try! They soon figured out this doe wasn't much of a "dear" after all. The matching bronze buck to the pair was "taken out" and lying on its side on the lawn complete with broken antlers. I thought animals knew better.

Yet another evening, when I had fallen into despair over the stillness at the property and was missing my dogs Stubbs and Scully that Cab had taken for a couple days, I was visited on the hill in front of the property by a fawn deer about the size of my dog Stubbs. I caught its silhouette through the family-room window as the evening grew dark. It was sitting, as Stubbs does, with its legs extended out in front, looking straight at me. I went to the outside deck and looked for the other family members. They were nowhere in sight. I went back in to lie on the sofa and watch a movie. The fawn sat there the whole time until I went to bed. It felt as though it was saying: "Don't worry; I know you miss your dogs and feel alone, but I am here and I want to comfort you." What a gift. I went from a feeling of sorrow to a feeling of appreciation and joy for this amazing experience that reminded me there is still hope to be had. I took it as a sign. It felt like God spoke to me through the deer that he is watching and has not forgotten me. I really wasn't alone. The weight on my heart was lifted. Yes, this property was a little slice of heaven.

After a bit of research on venue rates, I quickly learnedI had a commodity that could fetch thousands of dollars for one day of rental use. This propelled me into a radical renovation of the property, including removing all personal items such as photographs, clothing, jewelry, and memorabilia and setting it up for large scale use. I eliminated some furniture and opened up living spaces to accommodate more people. I also created a bridal suite in a detached guest house complete with a full length mirror, bridal vanity, including bridal emergency supplies like stain remover, safety pins, and a steamer for the bridal gown. The bridal suite featured a living room, bedroom, full kitchen and bath. Wedding photos hung on the walls, delicate quilts on the bed, flowers and lavender scented candles and soaps were a standard. The bonus room of the main house became the groom's room—very masculine with a pool table, bar, and outdoor cigar lounge—the groom's loved it. I referred to treating bride and groom the same, as an equal opportunity venue.

After I set up the property for use, I created a venue rental contract, hired a catering company, venue coordinator, and publicist. I also took out liability insurance under my corporate structure that was in place for the vineyard. Additionally, I had business cards, brochures, and a website created. It was up and running in about two months. As soon as the website was up, and some press releases went out, the news travelled of the new venue in Orange County throughout the event industry, and the phone started ringing off the hook.

The venue started to take on a life of its own. It was self-sufficient too. It was as though it wanted to be a venue. It was proud. It spread its wings and soared. Maybe it was my spirit manifesting itself when I couldn't see me anymore. I was there—all around, and one with the venue—my soul orchestrating the journey, the pipes my bones, the water turning into wine, my blood—no disrespect to Christ that tells us to drink wine to remember him. There was always something new I needed to run the venue. In the movie, *The Godfather* they go to the mattresses; I went to the garage. Anything I needed magically appeared in there. Extra extension cords, no problem. A battery for a generator, a wagon to transport supplies, anything and everything was there. The venue was living on its own life support—and the vineyard was proof that it was alive.

The vines were maturing and some were showing signs of fruit in their second growing season! There is a God! Chefs were calling and inviting me to their restaurants to sample cuisine in an effort to earn catering business. Life was getting a little more tasteful. We're not talking leftovers here. I felt like a queen for the day. I worked regularly with Mary from Jay's Catering. She often asked the chef to prepare something special for me when I met with her during planning meetings. It was a four-course meal paired with wine. Mary knew wine. She nailed the pairing every time. I felt insignificant at this time in my life, but I was treated like royalty within the event industry.

My publicist, Angie, put together an invitation for wedding professionals inviting them to the opening reception for the new venue, which included press coverage and interview with the venue manager. I had given myself this title, so as not to disclose my identity as the owner. I wanted to be in a better position to be the "bad wine" with renters. I was interviewed and featured in the Register newspaper in an article titled "A Rich Retreat That Can Be Yours For The Day" including an online video interview. That reception later led to hosting an

MTV reality show segment at the venue. Soon Bravo and others were seeking out the venue for use and the wedding bookings began. I met new people in ways I never imagined. My venue coordinator and I would proudly play music by Andrea Bocelli and Sarah Brightman when giving tours of the property to perspective brides—a passport to Italy. The emotion paired with the ambiance brilliantly. They may have missed the title "Time to Say Goodbye"—which was a good thing.

The weddings at the property were surreal. If you didn't know any better you would think you were in Europe, attending a destination wedding. I clipped lavender, field greens, and wild flowers from the grounds of the property and made flower arrangements to dress up the interior on the wedding day. The professional relationships I established along the way carried me and offered great synergy. The weddings and events we created were deeply rewarding for me as a result of creating unique and memorable experiences for others—one of my passions. Finally, the property was filled with the love it deserved.

The venue also offered something special—Waggy Dog Vineyards wine. After initially purchasing the property, Cab and I invested in cases of surplus 2006 Cabernet Sauvignon unlabeled wine called "shiners" from a vineyard in Paso Robles. The intent was to get our label out on the market until we could offer estate grown wine. I did not yet have licensing to sell the wine, but I created a cult following from donated bottles to venue renters and friends. I would inscribe a label on the bottle with a gold-leaf pen. The bottles looked unique—people loved them, and the wine was divine. By 2008, it was very drinkable: mature, and full bodied, with an expressive bouquet, fleshy with bursts of ripe blueberry, subtle hints of dark chocolate, a hint of sweet spices, voluptuous with a creamy mouthfeel. I felt really spoiled drinking this wine through the recession. I drank, shared, or gave away about twenty cases in two years. I didn't know it was going to be a currency in the near future until one dark day. You probably know this day too.

I was on my way to the bank to deposit a check and run some usual errands like grocery shopping, to fill up the car with gas and send mail from the post office. The money I had was sitting in a money-market account. It was kept there to earn interest until it was needed. Each month, I wrote a check from the money-market account to deposit into my household checking account. This day, I received a call from Cab while I was en route.

He said, "Don't write any checks from your money-market account. It is frozen."

"Frozen?" I replied, "As in, I can't access money?"

"Yes," he said. "I will let you know when you can."

This was the beginning of the financial meltdown in our banking system. I had about twenty dollars cash and my household account was on empty. I was also out of groceries at home and gas in my car. I was really caught at the wrong time for this. But, of course, there would never be a good time.

Scared to drive the car much more, out of fear of running out of gas, I drove back home and assessed my situation. Great, the dogs have food. My refrigerator was bare, however. I'd live on wine before eating the dog's food. What luck I had recently emptied the fridge to make room for the caterer for an event. The only thing I had edible in the house was pancake mix, orange juice, a few condiments, applesauce, nuts, some liquors, wine, maple syrup, jam and sugar. Hmm, where were those leftovers when you needed them? I'd even settle for the steak dog bones.

The next day, I had a scheduled meeting with an Italian chef, his cousin and my venue coordinator to discuss menu options and ways to market the venue. I usually served something to eat since the meeting went for hours. It's kind of the Italian way—no? What to do when life gives you pancake mix? Make pancakes! Oh...and they were pancakes to remember. I used the orange juice in place of water and some orange liquor in one batch. Yet another had blueberry jam on top with powdered sugar. And then another had applesauce as a topping and nuts. I arranged them on the kitchen island on different level plates and the pancakes were served. No one needed to know what was going on. I told my venue coordinate a couple of years later. Got through that day, now what?

The situation got worse before it got better. The money-market account remained frozen longer than expected. Cab started giving me some money each week to stay afloat with food and gas and some essentials while we worked through our settlement agreement and I waited for my money-market account to be available. I only had to eat pancakes for about three days. At least I didn't go hungry—bloated was another thing. Too bad I couldn't add some of that pancake mix to my bank account.

Without access to money, it didn't take long to get behind in the house payment and other bills. Soon I had to turn down event bookings because I could not guarantee that the property would not go into foreclosure by the time the event date came around. I couldn't risk someone's wedding or other event on my financial situation. Brides were very disappointed. Had I been able to book the events with certainty, I feel confident I would have secured the property indefinitely. I kept trying to come up with ideas on how to save the property but I had squeezed about the last idea from my bottle.

Didn't I have credit cards to access you wonder? No. The remaining credit lines on the cards were cancelled as a result of a mortgage late. I learned of this when I went to put gas in the car; the cards no longer worked. All of my available credit was gone, placing me in a cash only situation—I was not alone. I did, however, apply for a loan modification with my mortgage company. It was approved which took the property out of foreclosure, and reduced the monthly payment. It didn't take long to get behind again. As I closed real estate business, and generated venue revenue, I sent in money to try to stay out of foreclosure. Just about everyone, unless you lived on another planet, was in the same barrel and it was getting crowded.

I owed everyone, and without access to savings, credit lines, and my business down, I had a hard time paying bills. That's when Waggy Dog Vineyards wine became a currency. My gardener graciously accepted wine for payment for his services for a month. My CPA was paid with a case for tax preparation. My venue coordinator traded beauty services for wine. This wine was liquid gold, I'm telling you. Too bad I couldn't pay my mortgage with it. If I could have secured the property for a little longer, I would have captured the next wedding season of venue business.

Ironic that the house was never really a home that a happy family lived in, but it housed plenty happy families on wedding days. To me, it was more like a canvas that I was able to paint on with all my creative passions. It was an expression of me. It had my personality—maybe even my soul. I know my heart was in it. It was most likely the Viking Range in the kitchen that was always pumping out food, especially pancakes. The property exuded my love for entertaining, cooking, wine, decorating, and creating unique and memorable experiences for others. I decorated it. I maintained it. I pruned the vineyard. I dressed it up in wedding attire on the big day. I scrubbed the driveway, washed its windows, and cleaned it up after a big rain. It was my baby. It was a big baby and I was a full-time mom. I don't think, in hindsight, I ever really owned it. I think it owned me. It didn't want me to leave it either even though it seemed all grown up and self-sufficient.

Every time I thought the bank was going to auction it off after they assigned a sale date, it would get postponed a few days prior. I moved out when the first sale date was scheduled. I never imagined the bank would continue to postpone the sale date for a year. I felt like I abandoned my baby. I needed closure. It was difficult to watch it die a slow death from a lack of maintenance. I checked on it periodically. It was difficult emotionally to see it empty, abandoned, and hollow and I started to wonder if it was going to die on the vine.

A water leak developed, running up a bill of a thousand dollars a month. I had to shut off the water. I couldn't afford to troubleshoot the issue or pay the monthly bills. I had to wonder every day if the vines were going to make it. Fortunately, it was the winter season when vines are dormant. The vines had a new mom now and her name was Mother Nature. I felt like praying to Mother Nature: Please water my vines. Please turn the water into wine. I had done the best I could for the vines. It was no longer in my control; the fate of the vines was in someone else's hands now.

Before I moved from the property, I had a vine-trimming party with a few friends. This was the last I could do to prepare the vines for the next growing season. There were about eight of us, all together. I gave a crash course in trimming and we each chose a row to trim. One friend had a job just to serve us wine and keep the music going. Our music of choice that day was U2 and Led Zeppelin. Friends asked me why I was making such an investment of time and energy in a property I was destined to lose. I felt the vines deserved to achieve their destiny no matter what. I didn't want the time I spent cultivating the vineyard and laboring over it for three years to be in vain. I guess it would be difficult to relate if you hadn't spent the time, money, and energy on it. I was hoping to see the luscious, plump burgundy fruit on it in the next harvest season. This would give me some satisfaction that something ended on a positive note. Unfortunately the bank foreclosed on it before the next growing season. I never went back to the property. I can't bring myself to ask around if the vines made it. I'd like to think they did.

When I could no longer go back and see my baby, it hit me. It was really over now. There were no more harebrained ideas to subsidize it. I had given it a good fight. I was tired of trying to think of ways to save it. I had not relaxed into the loss and accepted the inevitable. I was still holding out for a miracle. That's when the grieving began. In some ways, it was less heavy to carry the worry of it like a ball and chain around my bottle trying to drag something that was too big and never going to happen. It was weighing me down emotionally. Sometimes when I left my apartment, I moved to and ran an errand I found myself making a wrong turn in the direction of the property when en route to go home. I pulled over and cried, "I want to go home." My home was gone, but I was lucky. I had a place to live. Not everyone could say that. I counted my blessings.

DOWNSIZING AND THE CHAIR THAT WOULDN'T GO

"Wino Forever"

Johnny Depp (The tattoo once read 'Winona Forever'!)

When it comes to downsizing material possessions from life, I came to realize that less is more. Without a doubt, there can be a certain amount of creature comfort in material things and emotional comfort tied to gifts received, souvenirs, and those carefully selected purchases. When you consider all the investment of time, energy, money and circumstance it took to acquire items, it can be grounds to want to hold on to them. Or you could be of the mindset that you associate the items with your failed blend and you want to throw everything out with the old bottle. These are two extremes, and there should be a good balance.

I found letting go of the household items I retained during my divorce was a slow process. I wasn't ready to completely dismantle my possessions initially and start over with a clean slate. Downsizing from a large property to a smaller one required that I make some decisions regarding furnishings and household items. My first transition to a smaller property resulted in holding on to too much. I felt the transition might be short-lived and I would be back to a larger property in time, so I rented two large storage units and started paying rent for furniture I wasn't using. Prior to storing the furniture, I separated everything in the house into a few categories:

ITEMS TO GO TO MY NEW PLACE: The size dictated what I took. Basically the essentials like enough furniture to be comfortable, enough dishes for the kitchen, some basic accessories, and artwork. These items were what worked, not necessarily my favorite items.

ITEMS OF VALUE TO SELL OR CONSIGN: These were items of significant value that I felt were too expensive to give away or donate. I chose a nearby furniture consignment store to sell them. They sent someone out to inventory the items and later a crew came and picked up everything with a large truck—very turnkey. Did you know you can consign good pieces of clothing through a clothing consignment shop? Perhaps I could get more selling items on my own, but the time investment was not worth it to me. It was a blessing to have the proceeds of the sale come in the mail in the form of a check each month. These checks paid light bills, grocery bills, gas, and basic essentials. On occasion, I splurged with dinner out or bought something.

ITEMS TO STORE FOR FUTURE USE: I moved to a place where appliances were included, but I knew if I moved again it might not be the case, so I kept my refrigerator, washer, and dryer. I also kept my professional Viking Range. If I gave it up, I felt it would be too expensive to buy back, so I stored it. Additional items were photographs, sentimental gifts, and items from childhood.

ITEMS TO DONATE THAT FRIENDS OR FAMILY DID NOT WANT: What do you do with things no one wants and the consignment store won't take? Donate them. You get a great tax write-off if you donate properly. In some cases, the dollar savings in taxes is more than what you would receive if you have a garage sale. It's faster and easier. Don't forget to get a receipt for tax purposes. If you are unsure of the amount to claim—you can get a book titled It's Deductible, which establishes the guidelines the IRS will allow. Goodwill or Salvation Army accept donations and can be good places to start.

I moved several times over the next couple of years. Some-times it was to another property I owned until it sold, or I tried a couple of different leases until I landed at the coast after a series of transitions. This was the first location I really felt at home since living in Trabuco Canyon. I was still working with the small bit of furnishings I had moved to my first new place, yet as I looked at them, I felt old energy attached to them. Each piece seemed to carry different emotional baggage tied to it. One of the pictures had wedding undertones to it and reminded me of my vineyard property.

Yet another reminded me of Cab because I had purchased it for him for Christmas. He must have understood this concept of emotional baggage early on. It showed when I took ownership of one of the rental properties he lived in after the divorce. He left many of the gifts I had given him over the years in the house. They hit me like a bottle over my head as I discovered them one by one when opening drawers and cupboards. The painting was left hanging on the wall. Not sure if he really understood this concept or wanted me to have the emotional impact as hard as a bottle over my head. At any rate, I got to a place that I felt I was surrounded by memories of a life gone by. My new place along the coast had a beautiful location with a view, but it was not providing a fresh, comfortable, uplifting space that fit the location. So what did I do?

I called the consignment store and had just about everything in my apartment picked up to sell. The money it would generate would provide a redecorating allowance. I looked through some magazines and found a few pictures of interiors that appealed to me and made a decorating vision board. I later went back to the consignment store and found a piece I was looking for—a beautiful white-tufted leather sofa. It became the central theme to a new contemporary look I decided to decorate in and perfect for a small place at the beach, cool, feminine, and comfortable. A few pictures of the ocean, boats, and blue skies, and I had my uplifting space! My dog Stubbs got new uplifting spaces too—fluffy new dog pillows and contemporary quilts for the sofa for him to lounge on. Now where do I store the wine, and what am I going to do to create the ambiance?

I placed aromatherapy candles strategically balanced in each room to provide ambiance without the lights on. Sitting at night with candles lit overlooking the Back Bay in Newport Beach with a glass of wine is my Zen moment. As for storing the wine, turns out I drink it faster than I can store it. You really can create a special place out of a small place—I had my doubts. Home is a place that should comfort you and your family. Too bad I can't live in a barrel forever safe and warm with plenty of wine. I guessed it was time for me to make the best of what I had to work with. As more of my consigned items sold, I added more and more comfort to my space with the occasional splurge on flowers, scented oils, and luxurious bath products –after all, it's all about me now!

So, how long did it take, anyway, for the items to sell? It took about five months for my originally consigned items to sell with the exception of one item. I was down to one item and it wasn't selling. This item had a long history attached to it. It was a chair. Cab and I had just purchased our first home. This was about twelve years ago. I walked into a furniture consignment store looking for accessories when this chair caught my eye. I wasn't there for a chair, but for some reason I loved it and had to have it. It was an antique chair from the forties with floral tapestry upholstery. I admit it looked like a chair a grandmother belonged sitting on. It was $20. When I brought it home, Cab was less than impressed and would have preferred the chair found another home. I blended it and it became that extra chair when you needed it. A sort of outsider chair but always there when you need it chair. It was one of the items I wanted to keep in my transition. Not a chair to consign and not a chair to give away, donate, or store—a chair that goes with me where I go, and it did.

When I moved from place to place, the chair went with me—a two-for-one special. The chair and I were a package deal. Sometimes friends would ask me: "When are you going to get rid of that ugly chair?" Then, before I moved to the coast, I thought it might be time to part with the chair and more of the old baggage. I also had too much furniture for the space. So, I reluctantly gave the chair to the consignment store to sell. Frequently I'd visit the consignment store and there it was, sitting like an old friend in the store. Hey, I know that chair!

After the chair was discounted, it still had no takers. I was called to come get the chair or the consignment store was going to donate it. I went and picked it up. It is now blended perfectly into my place on the coast. I sit on it every day at my desk. It has a nice oversized seat and comfortable frame. It's back, this chair of mine. It was more useful than I originally thought. No longer an outsider chair—now front and center. Now that I think about it more, it is the one thing other than Stubbs that has been the most loyal and around for every twist and turn. Maybe it's time for a "facelift" maybe give her a new look—a sexy chair makeover. After all, she's always been a chair only a mother could love.

Even chairs can re-invent themselves; it's all about being comfortable in your fabric and finding new purpose.

LETTING GO ALLOWS US TO GROW

"Accept what life offers you and try to drink from every cup. All wines should be tasted; some should only be sipped, but with others, drink the whole bottle."

Paulo Coelho, *Brida*

I used to think I was in control of my world. If I rolled my sleeves up and worked tirelessly I could make all things possible. I wasn't afraid of hard work. But really, does life need to be this hard? Sometimes the path of least resistance is the road to be on. I used to force my agenda and not take no for an answer. A huge ego coupled with a driven mindset. This mindset started to change as I started letting go of the things I could no longer control. The divorce was teaching me about releasing my will and embracing natural timing. Things do not always happen when we want them to; sometimes things happen when they are supposed to.

The details of dismantling our financial structure and assets became a daunting task. I did not have the financial resources to settle all of my financial affairs and get my financial house in order. The stock market took a big bite out of my cash reserves. It was going to be a slow clean up and recovery. Sometimes I would have huge real estate deals that were going to close and plans to pay off a creditor and the deal would cancel last minute. Constant struggles and disappointments became part of everyday life, but I was always provided for, thank God.

One month, I was short for my house payment and an unexpected check came in the mail from an accounting error of a bank account closed over a year ago. When I needed something to run the venue, it turned up, perhaps in the garage, something I forgot I had. With each of these gifts, I felt rich, blessed, and provided for, and I was financially destitute.

Hitting rock bottom and only having blind faith to run on released me from the burden of carrying the financial pressures of the past on my back. I had to let God carry me. I had no other support system in my life. It took a while. My nature was not to rely on anybody but myself, but I finally surrendered and relaxed into the loss, did what I could, and waited for answers on the things I could not fix at the moment. I didn't die. I was liberated.

Letting go taught me a valuable life lesson. It was important for me to realize that I am not in control. Only then could I embrace what is and what should be. I needed to learn to wait for the answers to come and live life in its natural timing. Timing that was not forced by my will, but provided for naturally. I realized I had viewed my life in terms of what I had created and how I chose to perceive and measure it. I was missing out on a deeper human and spiritual experience. I did not recognize the spiritual battle that was going on inside me. I was wrestling with my will to be done and missing out on a richer life experience.

I believe we have an inherent purpose to our lives, and if we get our ego out of the way, our destiny will unfold. And this life is more fulfilling and comes easier. Doors open when the timing is right. You don't have to beat them down. All of our experience prepares us for the journey and seasons us for our destiny and purpose. Letting go of control and relaxing into the loss initially felt like I was jumping out of an airplane without a parachute, but then as answers came, my faith grew and I began believing and trusting that I was not only going to make it, I was going to enjoy the adventure of the journey—an exhilarating ride I had never been on. The closest thing to jumping out of an airplane I will probably ever know—but never say "never"!

My life circumstances forced an awakening of my spiritual self. It took this magnitude of loss and life change to break through my ego. I found an undernourished part of my being. I became hungry for more enlightenment and understanding. I was learning a new way of living and relating. Yes, God, you are in control. Thank you for taking the reins, and for setting me free on a new life path. I hope I am always enlightened enough to stay the course of my highest and best use and destiny for which I was created.

RECOGNIZING THAT GOD IS CARRYING YOU

Make a list of those times in your transition that you experience an unexpected gift. It could be in the form of a call from someone with an encouraging word just when you need it or assistance. Perhaps the strength and courage you feel to face another day, which is a gift in itself. Keeping track of the gifts you receive and reflecting on them will act as a constant reminder that you are blessed and being provided for and not alone. You will also be able to experience the gifts over and over again. You might even start to recognize the miracles in life.

THINGS WE CAN AND CAN'T CONTROL

Make a list of the things you can control, and a list of the things you can't, and recognize the difference.

Things I can control in my life right now:

Things I have no control over in my life right now:

Ask yourself: "Does it make sense to stress over the things I can't control?"

NURTURING IS PART OF WINEMAKING

"Fine wines require fine wine makers."

Anonymous

Winemaking requires love and respect, nurturing, vision, and a supportive environment. There is science in winemaking that goes hand in hand with the creative process. The winemaker has to respect the science behind winemaking before he or she can impart the creative process. The winemaker starts with a vision of the characteristics and performance of the finished wine, then assesses the resources for the vision, utilizes science to cultivate the vision, and applies love and passion to the fine-tuning of the wine for the delivery of the vision.

While you are in the barrel playing the role of the winemaker, you will need to love, respect, and nurture your mind, body, and spirit within a supportive environment to allow your refinement process the ability to impart the creative changes it needs to deliver your vision and the new you upon release. This is a time for ultimate self-love and care. Give your mind, body, and spirit what they need to carry you through this journey—neglect one of these areas, and the others are not as effective because they are interconnected.

Divorce, grief, daunting tasks, and all the responsibilities in your life can deplete your energy and emotional reserves. You are at risk to overdraw your reserves and become bankrupt if you do not take the time to make deposits to keep yourself in balance. You are at risk to weaken your immune system and become prone to a host of ailments. It is important to identify ways to maintain our entire beings, especially now.

Winemaking is fragile and interdependent on a series of processes—some are natural and others are in the care of the winemaker. God created these beautiful grapes, but he gave man free will to create wine out of them. Your body, mind, and spirit are your God-given creation. Care for your entire being properly, so you can apply your free will to create your best experience to fulfill the destiny for which you were created. Create a nurturing plan for how you will care for yourself. If you establish a plan early on, it can act as preventative care, so you hopefully don't pop your cork, become corked, or crack your bottle. Remember, wine needs to be stored properly. You need to create a nurturing plan. This plan should be the first thing you accomplish on your to-do-list. If you take care of yourself you will be able to make better decisions, care for others, and deal better with the increased stress you are taking on. It will assist in helping support your overall health and wellbeing. Nurturing yourself should be your top priority. You can meet some of your own needs independently; other needs will be supported by professionals identified in your divorce support system and perhaps family and friends.

NURTURING PLAN
PHYSICAL, EMOTIONAL, SPIRITUAL

PHYSICAL: What are you willing to commit to doing to nurture your physical health? Here is a list of things to consider:

1. See your primary doctor for a check-up
2. See a wellness doctor for a preventative health plan
3. Take a brisk walk before work, or on your lunch hour
4. Take vitamin supplements
5. Drink plenty of water
6. Stretch throughout the day or try yoga
7. Start a fitness program at a gym, swim, bike, run, or all three, join a boot camp class
8. Take your pooch out and play fetch
9. Take the kids to the park and run around with them
10. Get enough sleep at night
11. Limit your alcohol
12. Take yourself to the spa for a massage, facial, manicure and pedicure

Now, make some PHYSICAL NURTURING commitments:

EMOTIONAL: What are you willing to commit to doing to nurture your emotional health? Here is a list of things to consider:

1. Consider a pet
2. Join a support group
3. See a counselor

4. Work with a divorce coach
5. Visit with family and friends
6. Join a church small group
7. Read books that comfort and uplift
8. Rid yourself of toxic relationships
9. Treat your ex-wine the way you want to be treated
10. Give more purpose to your life, help someone else in need
11. Do activities that bring you joy
12. Any of the physical nurturing commitments will support your emotional health

Now, make some EMOTIONAL NURTURING commitments:

SPIRITUAL: What are you willing to commit to doing to nurture your spiritual health? Here is a list of things to consider:

1. Meditate/pray
2. Journal your thoughts and feelings
3. Have a reading with a spiritual intuitive
4. Attend church
5. Commune with nature
6. Embrace your authentic self
7. Let go and let God
8. Become acquainted with yourself
9. Recognize your spiritual lessons
10. Take care of yourself and recognize your needs
11. Embrace some new learning
12. Respect your soul

Now, make some SPIRITUAL NURTURING commitments:

DIVORCE IS MORE THAN A PIECE OF PAPER

"The worst loneliness is not to be comfortable with yourself."

Mark Twain

Too bad divorce can't be a piece of paper you sign one day and then wake up the next in a happy new wine-life sporting your wine-colored glasses. It would be oversimplified to think of divorce the way the legal system defines it. We know all too well that a marriage blend has other physical and emotional contracts that bind and can be more difficult to sever. Long after the divorce is final, these other contracts could still be in force, however unenforceable, and no matter how hard you try to sever them, it takes time to heal and move on. Over time, these contracts become void. One thing is for sure: you have to work for a new wine-life. The postmaster doesn't deliver it to you with your divorce decree.

Loneliness can creep into your bottle and try to make a home inside you during your divorce journey. Try not to let it in; tell it you are enjoying drinking your own wine. There are a few good ways I found to run solo out and feel comfortable. Running solo, by the way, is a decadent lavish lifestyle that is all about YOU—you can get intoxicated drinking your own wine. Trust me; there is no excuse to stay at home alone when you have the opportunity and time to venture out. Activity will give you a break from your thoughts—a hall pass out of the barrel. After your break, the barrel will be waiting for you and might even feel good again, safe and warm.

Here is my list of favorites:

g alone, I pick an upbeat restaurant
ou can order food and drinks. Roll in
—confident, wearing a nice authentic
will do. Happy Hour is the best time
f wine: small plates and good prices.
rs if you like, and if you go when
d no one will know you are alone.
.e wine next to you. Don't forget to ask
.ey are from. Wine at bars range from the young
.re mature; you will fit right in anywhere hence the word "restaurant."

Movies – Can't find another wine friend to go? No worries. Anytime through the week, except for Friday nights, is good to catch a movie without feeling like its date night. Also, early showings on the weekend are a great time, an inexpensive escape.

Hotels – If you need a vacation and don't have time to take one, have a mini trip for an afternoon. Think about it, a lot of wine is traveling alone on business. You won't stand out. I would cover my bottle with my best dress and drive to the scenic Montage Resort in Laguna Beach. Drive in and splurge on valet parking. Walk in and pick the best table in the lobby and enjoy a glass of wine overlooking the ocean. Sometimes I'd roll my bottle around the manicured grounds and take in the sea air, and afterward, the live piano music in the lobby over yet another glass of wine. Sometimes I'd be there for four hours or more. Maybe I'd drop $40 bucks and I'd feel refreshed and rejuvenated afterward.

There are other ways to venture out solo, depending on what you like to do. Don't give up everything you've known because it was something you did with your ex-wine. Perhaps you can even do some of the things you used to enjoy before you gave them up while you were blended. Find time to reacquaint yourself with life through a new lens of possibilities. I suggest making a list of your favorite activities or you can once again use an online format such as Pinterest. Here are some examples:

1. Gardening – visit a nursery
2. Reading – visit book stores and public libraries, or take a book to Starbucks
3. Art – sign up for a class at a local community college
4. Cooking – sign up for a cooking class through William Sonoma

5. Photography – go out and take pictures on a nice day
6. Sports – Don't just be a spectator, jump in

When I felt loneliness creeping into my bottle, I joined a women's Bible study at Saddleback Church. I saw the same group of wine women weekly and the study was on "Love." Let's face it—if the love in your life is gone, we still need love. I needed to know someone else knew I was alive and still decanting. Maybe your children provide you with love, your friends, maybe your family, or pets. And maybe some of them aren't around or available as much as you need them. Connecting with others will help take the edge off loneliness. Maybe we have to love ourselves at times—enough to meet our needs by connecting with others or spending time becoming acquainted with who we are and what we enjoy doing.

Another way I connected with others was to enroll in an interior design program with the Interior Design Institute of Newport Beach. I completed a certificate in interior design. It was an intense program of learning space planning and choosing furniture, fabrics, and accessories. We even had field trips to Los Angeles to choose our items from the design center. I saw the same group of women twice a week and on field trips. I felt part of a group and I enjoyed learning something I was interested in that would be useful in my real estate career. I adapted the space planning design project for the final to my apartment when I transitioned from my larger property. Using furniture I had, but space planning around the layout of the design.

Sometimes venturing out is the easy part. Coming home and crawling into bed—alone—is the hard part. That's when my dog Stubbs got an upgrade. I ditched his dog pillow by night and let him have the foot of the bed. I like the sounds he makes when he sleeps. Those dog dreams and muffled barks were a welcomed change from the snoring I used to hear. I often wondered what could be stressing him so much in his dreams. Maybe he couldn't find his bone. Dogs, I found, are the biggest source of unconditional love. My dogs gave me purpose and joy every day. After Stubbs and I lost Scully his littermate, Stubbs became number one—no longer bossed around by his sister, the alpha dog. He didn't eat the leftovers from her anymore either. As a matter of fact, Stubbs and I shared special treats like a steak or a cooked chicken from the grocery store. I always had a dinner and sleepover buddy.

If you are in a position and have a pet-friendly, stable home and the capacity to care for a dog with walks and cleaning up, vet appointments, food, chew toys and bones, I would recommend rescuing one. This works best if you are transitioned and settled into a more permanent living arrangement. You have to be fair to yourself and the dog.

I believe a dog can help heal emotional wounds, provide companionship and support, love, and joy. My dogs never let me down. Stubbs is fourteen years old and still here with me! He teaches me patience, that it is a gift to wake up with the opportunity of another day, and that we need special care as we age. He delights in the simple things, always grateful and appreciative. He depends on me; he trusts me. He needs me. He is a gift to me.

I don't know much about cats, except they are a little less high maintenance for the most part, great for apartments too. Have you considered a cat? Companionship is good, even if it is the furry kind, and it can take the edge off the loneliness at home if you live alone. A pet can fill a physical space and bring joy into your life. They will always be happy to see you and you never come home to an empty place. No one hangs on every word you say better than a dog and tries so hard to please you.

In addition to the companionship a pet can provide, they can also aid in your emotional well-being. A pet is a source of unconditional love. They can bring tranquility to a space and have a calming effect, provide a sense of purpose, and take you for a walk if you let them. The Psychiatric Service Dog Society provides information on the use of service dogs to assist with the management of serious mental health symptoms such as bipolar disorder, depression, panic disorders, and others. See any similarities in a range of emotions you could be facing however temporary?

A pet can ground you. You might think you are rescuing them, but in actuality, you are rescuing each other. You're a perfect blend. Maybe they are capable of keeping our hearts from hardening as a result of leaving our hearts open to care for and love them, and open enough to receive the love they have to offer in return.

In time, your legal, physical, and emotional contracts will be a thing of the past. The emotional contract is the tricky one. An emotional contract can be kept alive by grief and unresolved emotions that hold you in bondage to the past. It takes up the space inside you to share with a new wine.

Not forgiving yourself or your ex-wine can keep the emotional contracts in force. I learned forgiveness was on the other side of blame or anger, and forgiveness did not mean I forgot. It meant I let the hurts go, so they didn't have an emotional stranglehold on me. When I had enough understanding to close the door of the past, I had the emotional capacity to open the door for the future. Forgiveness was the gatekeeper that permanently rendered the emotional contract null and void. You are not really divorced until all contracts are no longer in force.

MY FOUR LEGGED FAMILY

"If there are no dogs in Heaven, then when I die I want to go where they went."

Will Rogers

My dogs, Stubbs and Scully, were littermates. They were born on a sheep farm in Norco. Their mother was a working Border Collie sheepdog, the father a visiting Corgi. Don't ask me how that happened—I haven't figured it out. But I hear it was a roll in the hay—had to be, those Corgi legs never could have stepped up for the job.Stubbs got the long Corgi body with the short legs and when he wags his tail, his whole body wiggles. Scully was tall and graceful, more like a Border Collie. They both stole my heart the minute I brought them home at eight weeks. They have been my constant companions and family.

The dogs were in their senior years when I entered into divorce, slowing down and mellowing with age. They never asked for much, but they gave plenty. Scully was a mother hen. She was always checking on me, finding out where I was and who was on our property. She listened to every word with her crinkled face as she tried to take in everything I said to her with great interest, unlike her shorter-legged brother, Stubbs, who was always content to find a pillow and sit back and let others do the worrying.

The dogs were very in-tune to my moods and they always knew when to come over and climb on me or lick my face to try to cheer me up. Scully was like a soul mate. She could feel what was going on with me from far away and was always present when

I needed her to delight me with her affection and disposition. I loved to kiss her forehead between her eyes and give her a big hug. She would get so excited. She was a very sweet girl. Stubbs was always happy-go-lucky and took life as it came. He waited mostly for his sister to take what she wanted and he was happy for the leftovers. Scully picked the best time she could have to leave, any sooner, I would have been more devastated. She waited until I had a new relationship to carry me through the grief. I miss her every day. I am so grateful for her companionship and love.

I wrote a letter to her in my journal and this is what it says:

Scully you were my baby girl. You knew me better than I knew myself. You were so sweet and loving. You took care of me. I loved you more and more each day. My hope is that you felt the deep love I had for you and how much you were cherished and appreciated. I thank God for you and for the privilege of having you in my life. I will hold you close to my heart, love you forever, and miss you every day. I loved your kisses, your silky fur and kissing you in the middle of your forehead. I hope you had a happy life and always felt taken care of, safe, and loved. You were one of my favorite things about life and, on more than one occasion, you kept me going during hard times. Your devotion and unconditional love carried me through life's many challenges. I hope I did right by you. I am so sorry I did not see your physical aging as anything else but aging. I should have known you were sick. You were my precious baby girl. I hope I see you again one day.

– Love, your mom.

As for Stubbs, he is still happy, sitting close by on his pillow. Still happy-go-lucky, he grounds me every day, gives me purpose, and teaches me that life is sweet with simple things, and you don't need to sweat the small stuff.

AM I STILL DECANTING?

"You're not dead—you're dormant."

Cheryl Nielsen

Divorce and grief can compromise your day-to-day performance. I felt like a bottle of wine that was left open for a few days—flat and unable to perform as I once did. I wondered if I would ever be the wine I recognized, or if I was gone forever. Some of the alcohol in me seemed to have evaporated—I wasn't sure how to get a wine buzz anymore. Grief and heaviness from the insurmountable details of all the moving parts of divorce was decanting the life out of me. I feared I wasn't going to have enough body or a nose left in me to resemble a wine when it was all over. Either that or my fate was to become a Merlot—not a Merlot that drinks like a Cab, a "stinking Merlot." At least if I was a Pinot, I could have faked it better. With a divorce label on my bottle though, you can draw your own conclusions.

Everything became harder to do and took twice the time, so I started to doubt my abilities. I lost sight of me—no surprise now that I think about it—they don't put lights on the inside of barrels. What was left of me was in the barrel going through subtle changes, healing, and taking on new characteristics. Fortunately, what I came to realize is that I was not dead; I was dormant. I had to remind myself of what I was capable of. You can lose everything in life, but the wisdom of your experience—unless you pop your cork, but we're not going there. What you are capable of is still inside you and can be duplicated. This is the essence of who you are and it never goes away. After a refinement process, it will impart an even better ability to utilize it—rich with perspective, understanding, and new-found wisdom—your new wine is on steroids.

So you don't forget what you are cable of, make a list and keep it close. Read it every day if you have to—it will reaffirm what you already know and may have lost sight of. You might have survived cancer, childbirth, unemployment, the recession, years of Christmas holidays with in-laws, a few bad bottles of wine friends gave you. The list goes on. Trust me, there is a backbone in there somewhere and it's still supporting your weight. You really are still decanting.

UNCONVENTIONAL ROAD

"Hold the bottle up to the light; you will see your dreams are always at the bottom."

Rob Hutchison

Ever had an overwhelming feeling that you may have missed a red flag in your life when you begin to have a better sense of clarity of things you may have failed to notice? It appeared that I only had the radio station of my mind on one channel—the wine channel. I kept busy there, trying to earn money for the next bottle of wine. I was so good at keeping my nose to the bouquet that I overlooked the intuitive channel that was available to guide me. I realize I failed to take notice of some red flags and intuitive feelings telling me that all was not as it seemed. I felt like I had been wearing rose-colored glasses. Had I looked through my wine colored glasses, I might have seen better what was in front of me.

I had some unsettled feelings about people in my life and circumstances surrounding those people. I felt as though I needed better closure and understanding of my past. I did not want to make the same mistakes moving forward. I felt I was a mere student at using faith and my own intuitive guidance system in my life. I had not mastered the ability to interpret the signals of this new intuitive radio channel. It doesn't always come in as clear as I would like. I am trying to get better reception. I wasn't sure how I was going to get the understanding or closure for some of my concerns, but I knew I was not going to be at peace until I understood a better version of reality than the one

I had. I guess I put it out to the universe because the universe answered—a source to assist me came into my life.

A wedding planner came to rent the venue for a wedding and offered me a referral to her spiritual intuitive. I'm not sure how the subject even came up now that I think about it. She described how this intuitive had the capability to see things in her life—things she may have missed. She also provided guidance for the future. So, off I went to meet her with an open mind, journal, questions to ask, and a pen.

My "readings" with this spiritual intuitive dunked me deep into the barrel of denial, and out I came, able to see, thanks to my instant wine-colored glasses. My intuition was telling me there were problems and deceptions with people around me. This reading validated my intuition. Gee, maybe I could see enough out of those rose-colored glasses after-all. The information she gave was a lot to take in. I didn't even need to ask any questions because she answered everything on my list before I opened my mouth to talk. I left the reading in a state of shock. She liked to refer to it as "shock and awe."

Unlike traditional therapy where it might take years to talk out and bring clarity to issues, one reading using this "intuitive therapy" found things I had brushed under the carpet , and red flags I had chosen to overlook that I may have never come to know. A life of denial was now a shocking reality looking at me in the face. I accepted the information, but maintained a degree of skepticism about its truth initially. I wanted to discount it and defend my rose-colored glasses, but as time moved on, I would find material evidence to support the information, and other times, the pieces fit perfectly together as I reflected on my past. Sometimes other people told me they were aware of something even if I didn't solicit the information. I think my mind and heart was unsettled, and I continued to work on finding answers to unresolved issues. I believe I would have found some of this evidence over time, or gained some of this understanding, but perhaps not all had I not awakened to the reality in this way. The price to pay was more emotional pain and one hundred dollars an hour.

It can be a bit traumatic to be presented with information that is emotionally shocking. You need to be in a strong emotional place to begin with, and even then, it might be more than you can handle. For anyone who works with an intuitive this way,

I would recommend having a licensed therapist help with the emotional trauma that could result in the form of shock and awe. Even though I was ready to reconcile and bring closure to the past, I realize, looking back, that I fell into my old pattern of not embracing natural timing, and forcing understanding in this way brought emotional trauma that was sometimes difficult to manage. It was like I allowed an emotional virus to come in and render me compromised. Would you want to know?

Some people may not want to know about things they missed in their lives that would alter their perception of reality. Moving on and not looking back might be a better answer. For me, I had to know a better version of the truth than the one I had. I felt unsettled and confused. I lacked confidence in myself for the future. At times, I fell into despair, feeling I was not getting anywhere in my transition and that life was never going to be any different than the stuck place I sometimes felt I was in. The balance between the shock and awe and the wonderful future I had ahead of me gave me hope and the motivation to persevere while I was closing my past.

It is important to note that our psyche will allow information to come in when it is ready, when we can handle it. Forcing it to present itself all at once is potentially dangerous. I feel I suffered from some of the symptoms of Post-Traumatic Stress Disorder. Yet even though these intuitive insights brought on emotional trauma, I still went back for more readings. I would process the information from one of my readings, wait a couple of months then go back for more understanding and clarity. The processing I had to do on an emotional level over and over again with painful information lead to a state of emotional deadness. I was like a bottle of wine that had been left out for days—there wasn't much signs of life in me, flat and unresponsive. I also had difficulty sleeping through the night. My concentration was diminishing and I couldn't remember where I put things. It took a while for me to heal. But I finally did. Afterward, I only wanted to rely on my own intuitive guidance system.

I woke up and said, "Enough is enough"—I'm running solo. My intuitive muscle was developing. I was starting to recognize and tap into my own intuition with more clarity. The radio channel was coming in clearer. I was ready to trust my own intuition. Enough of the intuitive training wheels, I thought. I had lost confidence in my ability to see the red flags in life after realizing I had missed so much. Going through these readings built my confidence back up as they validated the intuitive feelings I was sensing in myself. The readings became more of a confirmation and helped me practice using more of my own intuition in everyday life.

Working with this spiritual intuitive made me aware that we have a spiritual support system and we can manifest things in our life if we ask for them. We have an ability to tap into our spiritual resources of intuition and an enlightened consciousness for guidance and direction. By living our life in this dimension, we can align ourselves with our true purpose and recognize red flags along the way. Listen to your gut; test it out. It's not just telling you to drink more wine. It is important to note that a spiritual initiative is just a human, and although they may have a gift, the messages they interpret can be interpreted incorrectly. Don't take everything as an absolute. You have to expect a margin of error. It's okay; the important information, I found, gets through. Watch out for the fakes though.

Sometimes when you get far enough ahead in your journey, and you look back over your life, you see the connecting dots. Some may seem like mere coincidences while others seem like a perfectly blended experience—although at the time, you had no way of knowing the bigger picture or meaning. I can illustrate this in my own life.

A year before Cab and I unblended, he unexpectedly took the initiative to hire a private detective to find my biological father. Something I had talked about doing for years. He had not been a part of my life since I was two. I was repeatedly caught off-guard when people asked me about my father or my varietal origin. I didn't remember him, nor did I have a picture of him. Probably some washed up root stock I imagined, with nothing left to produce. I was, however, curious about our wine history, grape diseases, and roots. My mother told me I was half Swedish which suggests a white wine. That was about all I knew other than I was the result of an unwed pregnancy in the sixties. Later, I came to find out that my father had blended with two wines at the same time and both had half bottles a couple months apart. Neither one were aware of this. My mother raised me single, until she married my stepfather when I was five. My sister's mother gave her up for adoption. My wine father was starting to show a lack of character. We clearly weren't Cabernet Sauvignon root stock or he never heard of a barrel refinement process. I'm starting to smell a Pinot Noir, which gives me concern that I might be carrying a genetic predisposition. But who knows, I needed to find out.

The private detective found him after just a few short days. He called my wine father and reintroduced me over the phone. He was very receptive to seeing me. A short plane trip away and all my curiosities were satisfied in a single day. Turns out, the trip to Sweden won't be necessary. Denmark or Holland perhaps, since the family vine is made up of Danish and Dutch. I hope red wine is produced in these countries. But there was more! I had five half-bottle siblings to meet. Some of which lived within a few miles of me. Divorce had separated me from family and friends, but I had a whole new life ahead of me with family I had never known. I did not realize when they first came into my life they would be there to bridge the gap from my old life to my new life. The timing was perfect.

My first Christmas unblended was spent in Lake Arrowhead at my Uncle Andy's complete with a family. I walked into a Norman Rockwell painting. More family was present than I had ever known, including my father, uncle, aunt, sisters, brother, and cousins. None of which were in my life not more than a year ago. They were gracious, warm, and accepting of me. We were in a lake-front condo, watching the snow blanket the trees, with the smell of Christmas dinner in the oven my Uncle Andy was cooking up. We all took turns telling each other what we were grateful for. I thought people only did this on television shows. I was so happy to be there. It was my best Christmas ever. I lost family and friends, but God gave me a whole new family to be a part of. I visit my Uncle Andy, his wife, Jessica, and daughter, Sophia, and friend, Glenn, on a regular basis. Some of the times spent at my Uncle Andy's home have been the warmest and funniest times I've had with family. I realized, at the time, this was a very significant experience in my life. In hindsight, I realized what it took in advance to provide the timing I needed in my life. I never anticipated the greater significance it would have.

If you plan to see a spiritual intuitive, I recommend keeping a journal. Write down questions and answers and take as many notes as you can during your reading. Don't dwell on every word and read it constantly, tuck it away and bring it out from time to time. You always have choices to change your destiny by applying your free will. There are no guarantees offered to make the right choice in life either. Sometimes a mistake gives us just what we need—more understanding. I refer to it as door number one, door number two, or more doors. Enter through one door and you have one destiny, or choose to open door number two and yet another destiny. A little insight into the future, and I found it profoundly helpful to keep me pushing forward. The darkness of barrel refinement—that neither has a past or yet a clear future—could feel hopeless at times. The readings with my spiritual intuitive opened the lid of the barrel and let me see into the future. I knew I was going to make it. I had something to look forward to. My life was not over and apparently the best was yet to come!

SPIRITUAL GIFTS

"And the vine said unto them, Should I leave my wine, which cheers God and man, and go to be promoted over the trees?"

Judges, 9:13

Sometimes other wine would judge me for turning to an intuitive for understanding and clarity. Most religions will tell you to live by faith. Trust in God, and be patient, and the answers will come. It was no coincidence that I was referred to a spiritual intuitive. The answers I needed were provided to me in this way; I can't judge the source. I've learned that our intuition is in direct alignment with our higher levels of consciousness and who we are at the deepest level. It defies logic; its focus is on truth and it can shine light on our inability to see what is in front of us at times. You have to know how to listen to it, I've found, from inside yourself. It was a lack of confidence in my own intuition that led me to seek it from the outside.

I was also previously influenced to a great deal by my wine grandmother, Gladys, who was a devout Christian with a spiritual gift of prophecy. The Bible makes reference to this as the ability to edify and encourage others (1 Corinthians 14-3). She also had a gift of speaking in tongues. The Bible makes reference to this as being filled with the Holy Spirit and able to speak in a foreign language to minister to others (Acts 2-6). When I was a child, my grandmother would be in the kitchen preparing a meal and break out into a symphony of words that took me by surprise. The spiritual language of speaking in tongues was a regular occurrence and sometimes followed by a vision. I never understood the words, but she would describe, in great detail, something about the future—perhaps a house where we were going to move, the color, the yard, and other characteristics. Soon, for one reason or another, we were moving and the house we found was exactly as she described. Yet another experience was when I was ten years old.

My grandmother took me to a small church one Sunday. She started speaking in tongues during the service with great articulation and deliberateness—her voice strong with conviction. A man in the congregation stood up and told her that she gave him a message in his native language—an old Native American dialect. My grandmother did not speak that language although she did have some Cherokee in her wine roots. On yet other occasions, I accompanied her to the homes of other ministers and spiritually-gifted people who read for us, who had the gift of prophecy. It was always a prediction about the future.

When I was in my teens, I would come to witness yet another spiritual gift—the gift of healing. My mother was diagnosed with breast cancer and healed. She underwent the traditional treatments—surgery, radiation, and chemotherapy. How very difficult for a single women with three children. At the time, I did not know what a diagnosis of breast cancer could mean. I was naïve and bought into the thinking that doctors cure you with the right medicine. She had blood tests that monitored her cell count on a regular basis. After some period of time using traditional treatments, she showed no improvement other than the hope that a radical mastectomy caught most of the cancer. It had already spread to the lymph nodes and the traditional treatments weren't giving her a cure.

One day she decided to go to attend a service at a local church. It might have been like any other service, only this day a woman from the choir stepped out to give my mother a message—a message that she was going to be healed that day. Shortly after, she describes her experience as feeling a very warm energy come at the top of her head and slowly work downward to her toes. She then felt the energy leave her body. Like a warm energy cleanse. There was no doubt to her that she had experienced the gift of healing.

Her doctor later confirmed she showed no sign of cancer. She has been cancer free for over twenty-five years. Several years later, she was called out during a church service and told she had been given the gift to heal. She is now an active member of a healing team. I never considered my mother very spiritual or religious in her life, but anyone at any time can open up to an experience and be forever changed. She has been on a spiritual path ever since.

I guess these childhood experiences made me open and receptive to a spiritual intuitive. That and mere desperation to know I was going to survive the collapse of my life. I find it interesting that people can make great progress in their lives if they just do one basic thing—ask for it! Many times the right people appear at the right time to help us on our journey if we just maintain a desire to move forward and the courage to take the first step towards the future. With each step we embrace, we get closer to our divine purpose—the life that is uniquely ours, one that utilizes our talents, skills, and wisdom to create a rewarding and purposeful life. Nothing goes to waste. All of life's experience delivers the by-product of wisdom. The mistakes we make will act as a guide to redesign our path or teach us something.

WHAT IF I FORGET HOW TO BLEND WITH OTHER WINE?

"Wine is one of the most civilized things in the world and one of the most natural things of the world that has been brought to the greatest perfection, and it offers a greater range for enjoyment and appreciation than, possibly, any other purely sensory thing."

Ernest Hemingway, *Death in the Afternoon*

I wasn't sure if I was ready to be released to the market and drank after I came out of the barrel. One things for sure—It's no fun drinking your own wine alone. I knew I had to come out sooner or later. I needed feedback from others. What do you think of my bouquet? Did I come out too spicy? Did I over compensate with too much vanilla? What is my finish like? Am I silky smooth, or a bit coarse? What do I taste like—ripe berries or acidic? What is my character like? Do I have a better backbone? These were some of the questions rolling around in my bottle.

I needed a life plan and a marketing plan. Not only did I need to appeal to other varietals, I needed to find out what varietals appealed to me—my taste had changed. For some reason, my libido was in overdrive. Maybe my balance was off. Perhaps I needed to get my tannins tested. Maybe I needed some reassurance that I was still desirable and other varietals would want to drink me.

I was forty-five years old. I wasn't ready to date more mature wine. I'm not a fan of fortified wine (with the little blue pills). I had a lot of pent up sexual energy. I might crack some older wine's bottle, I thought to myself. I was walking around like a Pinot Noir predator, sizing up other wine wherever I went—even trying to sniff their bouquet while standing behind them in line at Starbucks. On occasion, I was even imagining what was inside their wine bottle. I would delight in checking out their labels and asking questions when appropriate like "Do you wine here often?"

Sometimes some of the wine around me in my life that knew me when I was blended would call looking for a tasting appointment. One even invited me over for his own pity party because he, too, was getting divorced. He thought we had something to wine about together. Fooled me! His wife was out of town visiting family and he lied and continued to decant me for weeks. He thought I was ripe for the picking. Who's the predator now? Seductive Pinot Noir; I should have known. He was tempted by the fruit of another and tried to violate the natural laws of blending. I struggled for a long time about whether I should tell his wife what he was up to. Then I met someone who knew this Pinot Noir, without knowing my situation, and she told me he was a womanizer and drank around, so I figured his wife was well aware. These types have blended improperly so many times they have contaminated their juice before it even gets bottled. I ran back into the barrel for a bit. It's scary out there. I wasn't ready to be released. There is something divorce transition will do to you I found. It will label your bottle with a message that the universe can read that says: "Take advantage. This wine is weak." Who you calling weak? I'm a Cabernet Sauvignon for heaven's sake. I've been re-processed, too, so I'm even stronger than before. Watch it! I'll hit you over your head with my wine bottle.

IT GOT FREAKIER BEFORE IT GOT BETTER

"There are thousands of wines that can take over our minds. Don't think all ecstasies are the same!"

Rumi

One day, I got a call from a man who had picked up a magazine with an advertisement from one of my real estate listings. He was calling from Beverly Hills. I identified myself as the real estate broker in the picture. He said, "I just want you to know I am looking at the most beautiful woman I have ever seen." Sure, I thought to myself. Don't you have access to the internet? Heard of porn? Have you had your eyes checked lately? Still he persisted that yes, he was "taken" by my mug shot. So, I let him go on for a bit and then he identified himself and told me I could Google him and learn more. He was a prominent interior designer.

I emailed him through his website and he responded. Interesting. I tried to find some tannins on him online, but he seemed pretty balanced. He asked me if I could meet with him and if we hit it off if I would be interested in flying out of the country with him for a design meeting with an affluent client. We would have the opportunity to explore the sights and participate in some "wine tasting" by all means! I gave great pause to this. We talked a few more times until my intuition smelled another Pinot Noir. I'm done with this character. Can't I attract something besides a Pinot Noir? He persisted over a period of four years with phone calls and emails. I never returned any response. I later found out he was, of course—blended!

On yet another occasion, when I found myself in emotional turmoil, I turned back into a sexual predator. Perhaps I should describe more of the symptoms as they played out. One day, Cab gave me the feeling of being invisible as he failed to wave to me as he passed by in his car. He saw me. There was other wine in the car with him that waved. It was something small, but it pricked a repeated wound that I carried around of feeling insignificant and overlooked. I turned into an emotional wreck from an overload of stored messages. Now, keep in mind, I was the responsible type of wine that always tried to live within my label. I didn't allow myself to make judgment errors. I was disciplined and operated with a high set of standards. I was no Screaming Eagle; don't get me wrong. But I prided myself on my character as any Cabernet Sauvignon should.

This day, I changed into my alter ego—a Pinot Noir. It's like my personality split right in two with the emotional upheaval. The sensible respectful Cabernet was no longer in control; the Pinot Noir took over. That evening, I went to meet a girlfriend who was also in the midst of divorce for a drink at a trendy bar. The minute I saw her I said, "I'm taking a bottle of wine home with me tonight if it's the last thing I do." Immediately to my right was a younger, less mature, man sitting next to me at the bar—a dessert wine— white and very blonde. I'm not really into whites, I thought, but I'm sure he would be easy to swallow. I commented on his label and asked him what region he was from. It didn't really matter. When you have that much sugar in you, it will disguise anything.

My girlfriend and I decided to go dancing at another bar across town. I asked sugar wine to come. He agreed. I drove. Sugar wine turned out to be a good dancer. We danced and exchanged a few kisses on the dance floor—a taste less than the average two-ounce pour. I got close enough to smell his bouquet. He would do. He was going to satisfy my out-of-control need to choke the essence out of some bottle. The three of us drove back to his car and he asked me over to his place for another glass of wine. You're the only wine I'm interested in, is what I thought to myself. Sure, I'll consider another glass a warm up.

When we got to his place, poor sweet little dessert wine was surprised to find a predator Pinot Noir seducing him. He was good with it though. It was the first time using a condom in more than seventeen years and it broke (no surprise). I didn't know the thresholds they could tolerate. I was freaked out for six months— I was told by my doctor it can take six months for some sedi- ment to register on testing. Testing showed I was sediment free.

I got lucky. The good news is that I did get the reassurance I was looking for—that I was drinkable and it seemed to subdue the Pinot Noir in me for a while. Thank goodness, my character has never resembled a Pinot Noir before. I'm not exactly sure how my emotional state compromised my judgment. I was not a wine I recognized.

I can't help remembering his last words: "Wow, I thought I was lucky enough to have another glass of wine with you." He gave me some good feedback to answer my questions. I had the confidence to stay out of the barrel and start a marketing plan. I saw him again four years later. He called me from out of the blue and asked me out for a drink. Unfortunately, he had corked. His packaging changed dramatically. I appreciated that I don't call him a one-night stand anymore. I can, officially, once again say I've never had one of those. It's nice to be dignified again. You really can rewrite history sometimes.

Ladies, keep your corks in tight (do as I say, not as I do). Don't get close to any corkscrews too soon. Know that you will be targeted for your vulnerability and they will want to throw you over a barrel. They might mistake you for a screw cap, which is easier to open. Remember you are anything but. Good bottles of wine take more time to open. Don't let them decant you all at once. Don't be too open too soon; it'll make you look cheap.

Trust no one, especially Pinot Noirs. That goes for you guys, too. Women can be extremely aggressive, even if it isn't in their character, as I have demonstrated. Don't worry, you won't forget how to blend with wine, it comes naturally and is written in the laws of wine making. Timing is everything. I suggest waiting until you are fully matured and released complete with a divorce decree, life plan, and first and foremost—a healed heart.

An unhealed heart is prone to re-injury and will disrupt your refinement process and set your timeline back to have a meaningful transformation to become the wine you want to be. If you release yourself too soon, you may run the risk of never being what you are meant to be. If you have an unhealed heart with cracks, they give open access to your soul. If you re-injure, the cracks will get bigger and you will need even more time to heal. Love can offer healing, but you most likely won't be in any position to know what is real and what is not. You also need to be free of your emotional baggage I like to refer to as "emotional viruses," so you can connect on a healthy level. Get your bottle examined to establish a current baseline of health before you blend.

EXAMINE YOUR BOTTLE

"If penicillin can cure those that are ill, Spanish sherry can bring the dead back to life."

Sir Alexander Fleming

In the early stages of divorce, I recommend establishing a current baseline of your overall health. If you have any current health issues, you want to address them sooner versus later. The increased stress of divorce can potentially weaken your immune system. You don't want your health to suffer more by the increased stress you are taking on. If you are given a clean bill of health, great, next is to maintain it and possibly even improve on some aspects of your physical health. See your personal physician for a complete physical examination and follow your doctor's recommendations for any further evaluations.

Consider testing for sexually transmitted infections (STIs), sometimes referred to as sexually transmitted diseases (STDs) or "sediments" in a Meritage Divorce. You could be carrying a sexually transmitted infection with no visible signs and not be aware that you contracted it in your seemingly monogamous marriage blend.

A sexually transmitted infection (STI) is an infection passed from person to person through intimate sexual contact. This contact can be in many forms. I'm not going to list all of them here—use your imagination—you should know what happens when two bottles get together. There seems to be a presumption that a condom will protect you from all STIs. Not the case. For one thing, condoms can break. Also, some STIs are spread easily by skin-to-skin contact. You'd need a full body condom, which doesn't exist.

Think you are not at risk? Think again. There are 19 million new infections each year according to the U.S. Department of Health and Human Services. Furthermore, newly divorced middle-aged women who sometimes feel they can no longer become pregnant and are not in the demographic to be at risk don't worry about using condoms. Take off your rose-colored glasses and get some wine-colored glasses before it's too late. Actually, the divorced pool of people having sex, and perhaps also a little naïve since they didn't concern themselves with this while married, are potentially high-risk carriers as a result of not practicing safe sex.

Think you'll take a pill and everything will go away? Think again. There are several that will be with you for life (unless a cure is found). We all know about HIV, but there are others that can be potentially life threatening. Take HPV for instance (Human Papillomavirus). Some sources estimate at least half of people who are sexually active will contract the HPV virus at some point in their lives. There are 100 or more types of HPV. Some types can cause cancer in various parts of your body. Ask your doctor about STIs, and ways you can protect yourself. In the case of HPV, It can be transmitted from skin-to-skin contact, so a condom is not a guarantee. At a bare minimum, use a condom.

If you plan on blending, why not ask them to see a doctor first and get tested for sediments? Then they can present a copy of the lab report before you go near them. Doesn't sound very romantic? Neither do any of these sediments. Perhaps a Pinot Noir would be taken back by this request, but hey, you don't want to cork yourself either.

EMOTIONAL VIRUSES

"And no man putteth new wine into old bottles; else the new wine will burst the bottles, and be spilled, and the bottles shall perish."

Luke 5:37
King James Bible (Cambridge Ed.)

I relate grape virus diseases with unhealed emotional wounds. Grapes can become infected with viruses that have the ability to take over plant cells and reprogram them to make more virus cells. These cells spread to all parts of the vine and remain with the plant for life. The symptoms can go visibly undetected or show up as a decline in productivity, or on the leaves, stems, or fruit. The plant is permanently compromised just like the psyche can be from traumatic childhood wounds. In some cases, if the trauma is so severe, a personality disorder can develop that could lead to emotional dysfunction. Other times, the wounds are less severe, but a virus enters nonetheless and places a stranglehold on our emotional make-up. The infection compromises our emotional intelligence, limits our beliefs on how we perceive ourselves and capabilities—visibly undetected and shielded from perhaps even our own awareness, it compromises our productivity in life.

If you start a new blended relationship and either you or the other wine is not healed completely emotionally from divorce—or unhealed childhood wounds—you are at risk of catching an emotional virus or being a carrier yourself. It's easy to catch an emotional virus when you are in a compromised emotional state. You meet someone and leave yourself wide open for infection. Soon their emotional virus has fused with yours and you are reprogrammed to fit their unhealed emotional make-up. You become the perfect host to repeat the dysfunction of the past. You will be warned of the danger ahead in the form of red flags, which are clues in someone's behavior signaling the presence of an emotional virus.

Let's face it, anyone can have emotional viruses that carry the dysfunction of the past, from painful experiences, but it is how they've dealt with those viruses that determine if they are contagious. If we don't want them to have a strangle-hold on us to define our emotional make-up to compromise our emotional health, we must treat them so they become dormant. Left untreated, you choose partners that are not healthy for you because you are not healthy either. The only way for you to rid yourself of emotional viruses is to work through the trauma that gave them to you in the first place. The resolution may lie in the science of psychology or spiritual healing. There are a number of paths—one path does not fit all—you may need to try a few before you find one that works. First, however, you must take a good look at yourself. The time you spend in the barrel refinement process gives you the opportunity to self-reflect.

You may have hit an emotional plateau in your marriage blend because you were blocked from your awareness of a virus you were carrying that compromised your ability to relate at the level the blend needed to sustain a healthy relationship. Perhaps you and your ex-wine were a dysfunctional blend from the start because your viruses were the perfect host to play out the dysfunction of the way you grew up or a dysfunction of your perceived value—a comfortable fit for all the wrong reasons.

I had an idea that Cab and I each carried some emotional viruses to the blend and, over time, the emotional health of our relationship died on a vine. He knew it, and I knew it. We tried to identify the issues in marriage counseling, but the focus was on the dynamic, not the underlying viruses. Cab's email he sent me to end our marriage conveyed his defeat. Here is his entire email:

"After this weekend, I came to the realization that we are broken and cannot be fixed. Even though I love you very much, that is not enough. I know I do not make you happy, in fact, just the opposite. I do not want to fight with you anymore. I am so sorry I cannot be the person you need or deserve. I know you are miserable and so am I. I think we need to discuss how we should end things. I am amenable to anything. I will be looking for an apartment today. I do not know what else to do, I give up." I returned the following response:

"I can discuss this with you kindly and without blame or emotional turmoil. This is a no-fault situation and I am not blaming you for our pain since we both were broken in many ways from our past before we came together. I would not like to damage one another any further and I would like to try to retain our financial assets and make good decisions. I am not going to point fingers and I want you to have the love in your life you are looking for. I take responsibility for my part and I would like to transition both of us in the best way we can. I am capable of being mature in this situation. I am sorry too, I agree, we can't come together, we are too hurt."

I believe the emotional health of our relationship eroded over time because our underlying viruses were compromising our emotional intelligence and ability to connect and support each other at the levels we needed to nurture, grow, and produce beautiful fruit to restore and replenish our emotional reserves. My time in the barrel refinement process revealed the patterns of dysfunction. I used the time to get in touch with my emotional viruses. I believe the divorce was a "wake-up call" that I was not living in line with my authentic self or loving to my full capacity. I was eager to not hold back the next time I found myself in a blend, in love with a new wine. I felt like I could see with better clarity through my wine-colored glasses I had earned through self-reflection.

IT MIGHT BE QUIET FOR AWHILE

"Gladness is taken away, and joy out of the fruitful field; and in the vineyards there will be no singing, neither joyful noise. Nobody will treat out wine in the presses. I have made the shouting stop."

Isaiah 16:10 (KJV)

As you spend time in the barrel in the refinement process, you might become disturbed by the isolation you may find yourself in. I found it surprising that after Cab and I announced to our family, friends, and associates that we were getting divorced, the phone stopped ringing. Hardly anyone called to express their regrets or offer any well wishes, for various reasons I assume. I concluded, over time, some were never really true friends; others didn't know what to say, while others knew the parties were over. I wish, just occasionally, someone would have dropped by and opened the lid to the barrel just to make sure I was still in there. It would have made such a difference. I know the loneliness of divorce all too well.Living in a rural area with no neighbors didn't help.

It sometimes felt like I had dropped off the face of the earth. It was so painfully quiet—it reminded me of what solitary confinement prisoners must go through. At night, it was just the dogs and me, and the frogs in the nearby creek making any noise. Many times, I went outside when it was dark, stood on the lawn, and gazed up at the stars and screamed at the top of my lungs in anguish of the stillness. My screams broke the silence and were therapeutic to some degree. I felt mildly better. Maybe I was hoping my voice would signal to God that I was barely holding on.

I kept busy with a multitude of tasks surrounding that start-up of the venue and marital settlement agreement I was drafting. That took my mind off the isolation, to some extent. I wanted to make new friends, but I had little energy for small talk. Short sales were sprouting up in the real estate industry and I was negotiating pay-offs with my client's lenders. This was all I had the energy for, outside the daunting divorce details. I was running exhausted daily. I missed having a normal life with the interaction of friends and dinner parties. Let's face it—I was desperately lonely and I didn't even realize I had fallen into a deep depression. That's when the drinking began.

I started drinking a couple of glasses of wine each night before bed, hoping to take the edge off, relax, and fall fast asleep. I didn't realize I was adding to my depressed state of mind. Then, one day, I thought my bottle was going to crack from the pressure I was under and all of me was going to spill out into a puddle on the floor. Permanent damage, too. How would I ever put the shattered glass back together? How long would it take for someone to find me and who would take care of me were my thoughts. I needed damage control. I called Cab and told him it was an emergency and asked him to come to the house. I thought I might be nearing a nervous breakdown. I was feeling like I didn't want to go on anymore. I told him so.

When Cab arrived, he found me sitting on the sofa in the family room. He walked over, sat down, and told me he spoke with our marriage counselor who told him that he should take me to a psychiatric hospital and have me committed for observation and treatment for depression. Our marriage counselor phoned me shortly and said it would be a good idea for me to go there and have a "good rest." He made it sound like it was a vacation. If I were to take a vacation, I would go to Italy—not the psychiatric hospital. Italy has wine and a few of my favorite things like red-blooded Sangeoviese—the ones you can love, and the ones you can drink while they are still young. Not to mention the salami, cheese, and delicious blood orange juice. For that trip, I could pack my bags and be at the airport pronto! But that offer wasn't on the table.

I wasn't going to a psychiatric hospital. I had venue appointments and client files to work on. I had a lot of open wine and it would all go bad if I didn't finish it. So I refused to go. In exchange, I had to report to a psychiatrist's office the next business day for evaluation. Our marriage counselor was on the hook for me and had to follow a certain protocol since he was informed of my "condition." He told my ex-wine I needed to be watched until I had the evaluation.

Cab sat on the sofa doing exactly as he was asked. He watched me like I was about ready to crack any second—very little dialogue and just a lot of staring. After an hour of this, he commented that he had dinner plans in Beverly Hills. Why was he bringing this up now was my initial thought, and then I had flashbacks to when I was a distraught teenager and my mother asked me not to cost her money to take me to the hospital. I felt he was saying: "I've got somewhere else I want to be and you're not worth my time." So, I told him to go, convincing him I would be okay. And so he did. And once again, I got the message I had already been carrying around my entire life: YOU'RE NOT WORTHY. This is why I never relied on anyone or asked for help.

That night was the roughest night of my life. Emotionally, I was just hanging on. It was a horrible feeling of trying to see any light in the barrel. I was exhausted from the pressure and losing hope I could continue carrying the load any longer. I had to get through the night and make a plan the next day—a save-my-bottle-from-cracking plan. I realized I had to take better care of myself. I also needed more emotional support. It was time to add a counselor to my divorce support system.

I decided to start seeing the counselor Cab and I spent many months with in marriage counseling. That made it easy for me to go in and immediately describe my current emotional and mental state. His first recommendation was to stop drinking alcohol, including my daily glasses of wine. I hardly considered it alcohol, more like water and a basic necessity. Besides, I still had things to wine about. But I didn't argue. He also suggested I get more physical exercise, and are you ready for this one? Start dating. It had been two years since Cab and I split and the divorce just needed to be acknowledged by the court. The agreements were already made. He was right: I needed to get my bottle out there and go on some tasting appointments. But first, I needed to whip my bottle into shape. I needed more bottle confidence. I decided to explore some fitness programs and work on my bottle while I was seeing the counselor for my depression.

WHIP THAT BOTTLE INTO SHAPE

"Age is just a number. It's totally irrelevant unless, of course, you happen to be a bottle of wine."

Joan Collins

My venue coordinator invited me to a Boot Camp class for women. This introduced me to the concept of "muscle confusion." Essentially this refers to using different exercises and movements in your fitness program. By confusing the muscles with constant change, they don't get used to a consistent program and prone to hitting a plateau. Celebrity trainer Tony Horton harnesses this concept with his P90X system. This is an at-home version of the Boot Camp I attended. I needed the class format to get my bottle out of the house and isolation I was in. I liked feeling connected to other wine I could see on a regular basis. I wasn't sure if I could endure the intensity of the program, as I was not in the best of shape. I nearly gave up on the first day. It was more difficult than I imagined. So I did what I could and hung in there, and within a few short months, I watched my body tighten and take on an athletic physique. I was in my forties, but I had never felt sexier. The physical activity dramatically changed my state of mind and feelings of hopelessness turned to hope and excitement for the future. I was hooked.

Some additional bottle confidence came from taking a few pole dancing classes. My friend Vinoo invited me to go with her to a class one day. Sure, why not, I thought. Who's going to know? It's not like I'm going to apply for a job later at a strip club featuring mature wine. I wasn't sure how my bottle was supposed to twirl around a pole, let alone wear a pair of stilettos, which I refer to as "ho shoes," but hey, I've worked through the impossible before. Turns out, it's not that difficult to twirl around a pole. But, climbing a pole—this gives me a new found respect for strippers. They actually have to work hard to be able to do this, not just rely on their sexy moves and bottles. The moves I learned I thought might come in handy one day if I ever found myself turning into a Pinot Noir. Hope the wine spectator can't see that well—illusion is sometimes better than reality. I guarantee the taste will be good though. Now, how am I supposed to get these tasting appointments?

Turns out, when you are sporting a fit bottle, the tasting appointments come to you. I dropped two sizes in my clothes from all the physical activity and changing my eating habits with a higher protein diet and complex carbohydrates. I quit eating bread and sugar all together. Remember, I'm not drinking either. I started taking vitamin supplements—a multi-vitamin, calcium, and fish oil. I felt like a new wine. I was a whole new wine, inside and on my label.

It was time to splurge on a few new pieces of clothing for my new bottle. The ones I had were in danger of sliding right off me. I took some pieces of clothing to a tailor to have altered to save money and invested in a couple of new dresses to wear on future tasting appointments. When I went to Starbucks for a break from work, I regularly had men stop in their tracks and open the door with noticeable eagerness and smiles. At first, I dismissed the attention as random acts of kindness and friendliness, but soon I realized this was different. Wine was responding to me in a different way than ever before. If I didn't know better, I would think some were interested in blending.

My confidence began to soar. I knew it was time to go on some tasting appointments. I felt ready to start drinking wine and blending with other wine again. I decided to make a dating plan. I knew I didn't forget how to blend after my encounter with Sugar Wine, but I wanted a boyfriend, someone to date and have a relationship with in an exclusive blend.

WINE DATING GAME

"Let us have wine and women, mirth and laughter, sermons and soda water the day after."

George Gordon Byron

The first thing I did was to list the characteristics I wanted in a wine to blend with. Pinot Noir definitely wasn't it. More like a varietal grown on European soil, I was thinking. After a couple of trips to Europe, I was attracted to Italian, French, and German wine that exuded earthy, masculine characteristics with a sensual romantic finish. Even the sweet white wines were becoming appealing and begging to be drunk.

One year after a return trip from Europe, right before Cab and I split, I had run across a German man during a brief business related encounter, but I remember my thought when I met him which was "Wow, what a beautiful sweet German wine. Who is the lucky lady who gets to drink him?" I took a piece of business literature with his picture and threw it in a pile somewhere amongst all the other business contacts and never gave it another thought. From his label and bottle physique, I can expand on my list a bit further and say, I wanted an educated wine, preferably self-employed, traveled, and athletic, likes to drink wine, cook, good sense of humor, opens easily, and has some maturity, but still spontaneous and adventurous enough to surprise my palate. Something sweet for a change would be nice. A tall order for a bottle of wine, but I knew it was out there. I had seen one before; I just had to look carefully and sample a few to find it.

The next thing I did was to try a few different paths that would give me access to wine. I couldn't limit myself to just wine shops and bars. I had to branch out and see where else they might be hanging out. I tried an online dating site without a picture. I did not want any of my clients to see me online. I quickly shut it down after I met a wine who lied about his tasting notes.

I then turned to social activities through Meetup.com. I chose things I was most interested in, like wine tasting, and outdoor activities. It was an excellent way to meet wine casually and more organically. It was a bonus when I made friends with female wine. I went on a couple of tasting appointments, but nothing had yet delivered the experience and characteristics I was looking for.

Next, I tried speed dating. You can learn a lot with a three-minute investment. The wine opens, hits your palate, and then you can spit it out. I enjoyed a few good tastes, but still haven't decided to buy an entire case of any wine.

I then joined a dating service that paired three female wines with three male wines for an evening over dinner. If you thought you might like to taste any of the wine, the service would let the wine know and set you up for a tasting appointment. I met a wine this way that I started dating. He was very close to what I was looking for. He was a younger Italian wine. After dating him for a period of time, I came to realize I was too insecure with the eleven-year age difference. He was a triathlete with a beautiful physique, and worked in my industry. We worked together, played together, but my mind kept telling me we were not a match. He was a good experience, but a little too immature for my taste. I broke it off and went back on the market. He landed another bottle very quickly I heard through the grapevine.

A few months later, I attend a wine-tasting event as a result of advertising my real estate business in the program. I planned to stay long enough to make sure my ad was printed. It was a beautiful summer day and the event overlooked the ocean at a hotel in Laguna Beach. I wore a lovely sundress with bright orange flowers with a cut that showed off my toned shoulders—one of the dresses I had just splurged on as a reward for my bottle transformation. As a result of advertising in the program, I received complimentary wine tasting, so I wasted no time to get in line for a glass of wine.

I wasn't taking in much of my surroundings, but as I reached the front of the line and my glass was being poured, I found myself standing next to a younger, less mature wine. Yes, I've developed a taste for younger wine it seems and I can't seem to break the pattern. I guess I didn't learn my lesson. He was wearing a European suit and shoes and had a label on him that signified a beautiful German-produced Riesling. Someone nearby used the word "divorce" in conversation and we both sighed aloud simultaneously. I looked at this beautiful wine and asked, "You, too?" He replied, "Yes."

We stepped out of line to a nearby table to introduce ourselves. His name was Maximilian. What do you know—I identified the wine nearly perfectly. I could smell it from his bouquet. He was German, blonde and blue-eyed and definitely a dessert wine. We had some common interests and we were both passionate about spending time in Europe. We tasted a few more wines, and as it got later in the evening, we became hungry. Max, as I began calling him, expressed an interest in getting some dinner together. The hotel restaurant was closing, so he asked me if I would join him at another restaurant—perhaps closer to home. I knew of a steakhouse and he suggested we leave to have some dinner. He had driven to the event with a friend in her car. He introduced the two of us and asked her (a blonde female Chardonnay) if she wanted to join us. She said "no" politely and continued interacting with the group of wine she was sitting with. This was the first red flag I missed. Later, I found out they were on a date.

So, off we went to the steakhouse down the street. My place was very near, so I asked if he wanted to stop and pick up a bottle of my unlabeled wine. He seemed excited to try it. I looked at this attractive young Riesling and only felt delighted for the conversation and opportunity to share a bottle of wine over dinner. I figured when we were done, I wouldn't see him again. I dismissed any interest he would have in me as a result of a ten-year age difference. It didn't work for me before, what would make this time any different? The thought did cross my mind that wine only gets better with age. Still, I had no expectations. At this point, I was enjoying being out and talking to him. I didn't feel worthy of him to desire more. Even though my bottle was in the best shape of my life and I was feeling better than I had in years.

I decided not to think too much with my left brain. This side controls the science of winemaking, not the creative passion of winemaking. Perhaps this would be a mistake, but I just relaxed into the experience. Honestly, I just wanted to drink him up—no sipping, more like guzzle. I was ready for some sweet wine. If any spilt on the floor, I would lick it up and not let any go to waste. I was getting intoxicated without even a taste. His bouquet was masculine, but delicate at the same time. He exuded an adorable boyish charm about him, which felt understated for his life experience. He had the most beautiful eyes that gazed intently at me as though to say he was interested in what I had to say.

When we passed the steakhouse, it was already closed which didn't leave many options. There aren't many choices in Trabuco Canyon aside from the steakhouse, Cooks Corner, and a Mexican restaurant. I couldn't take him to Cooks Corner, a biker bar, in a suit—the beer drinkers might want to toss his bottle out the door, and I had plans for him. I didn't want him to break. I wanted to spend more time with him, enjoying his charm. That left what was in my fridge for an option for dinner. Hopefully, I had more than pancakes to offer.

Upon arriving home, I immediately surveyed the leftovers in the fridge—chicken and sweet potatoes that should do. I opened a bottle of unlabeled wine and we sat at the bar in my kitchen. Afterward, we retreated to the living room where I shared a piece of art from Italy. I lit the candles for ambiance. We did not decide to kiss, nor was I expecting it, but we fell into a tender kiss in front of the fireplace and Italian painting. It felt natural, almost familiar to me, as though I had drank this wine for a very long time. It was something I was craving, but I did not expect to find it in a Riesling. I suddenly felt completely at ease and worthy.

It was the first time in my life I stayed up all night making love, which rolled into three days together. It was also a time in my life when I was completely comfortable in my own skin and more sure of who I was as a result of self-reflection in the barrel refinement process. The old wine never would have surrendered to this kind of unselfish lovemaking he bestowed on me. I asked him, "Why so much?" and he replied, "Because you deserve it." The euphoria that followed was something I had never experienced. Still, I had no expectations. I thought of our encounter as a one-time gift for me.

With Max, nothing was really thought of; we were like a current that flowed together. We blended so easily and fit together so well, there were really no decisions to be made. We became inseparable. We decided we only needed one bottle between the two of us, that way we could be closer. I dumped half of me out of my bottle, and Max poured himself in. Now it would be easier to spoon each other at night when we slept.

I was delighted to find that Max put our blend first. I wasn't a mere leftover thought. He demonstrated a desire to maintain it above anything else in his life. When he sensed or I shared I had something on my mind, he would run a bubble bath and toss my bottle into it. Naked and exposed, my label came off in the water. I had no way to hide in the bathtub. He joined me and we talked it out amongst the bubbles over a glass of wine. He didn't want any unresolved issues in our blend. He wanted to keep things smooth and tannin free.

We had an emotional intimacy like nothing I had ever experienced. I never had any wine work so hard to understand me or make it such a priority. He hit every note I wanted from my tasting notes for the wine I was looking for. He was fun loving, spontaneous, passionate, sexy, kind, attentive, spiritual, and a joy to be with not to mention sediment free. Maybe I am deserving of love and loveable. I want love. Love is possible again. When you are ready, love will find you so I thought.

THIS WINE IS TOO GOOD TO BE TRUE

"I pray you do not fall in love with me, for I am falser than vows made in wine."

William Shakespeare, *As You Like It*

The reality I was in started surfacing about six months into the blend. There were some instances that arose over Max flirting with other wine (in front of me) and online through social media. I think social media is an excellent way to keep in touch with your social network. I have rightly or wrongly always considered much of what wine posts to be a version that is less than what they are. I find some wines trying to hold up some distorted label and tasting notes they want the rest of us to believe when, in actuality, they taste nothing like what they say.

Max told me his Facebook personality was his alter ego. This ego resembled a Pinot Noir. That explained a lot. That was a little too much for me to keep up with. I wanted to keep things real and authentic. I have seen Facebook used as a virtual wine bar to play around in. Even if the flirting stayed in cyber space, it could cross the line and be a form of cheating, in my opinion. After all,if you arein a blended committed relationship, isn't it a bit disrespectful and a betrayal to show a network of wine that you are open to flirty and sexy talk with them in spite of your blended status? Doesn't that invite them in and give them permission to blend?

I watched as, countless times, Max exercised no boundaries. I also watched some of his Facebook wine friends became his clients. This one Pinot Noir had no intention of doing any professional business. She was interested in some personal business. And so she wasted countless hours of his time—or did she? I even found a birthday card that said: "Hopefully you will spend your birthday with me." Sorry, Pinot bitch, we have plans to go to Coronado for the weekend. I guess it doesn't look like it's going to happen. I thought he was an immature bottle of grape juice that didn't see traps in front of him. But I had to realize he had the most beautiful label and bottle and sweet bouquet, so it seemed plausible all types of wine would chase him without much encouragement from him. I dismissed any wrong-doing on his part.

Yet, other times, Max's status changed from "blended" to "networking" on Facebook. The red flags were once again waving. One time I logged in and found I did not have access to his wall—I was blocked. He claimed he blocked access because he didn't want any more upheaval in our blend or misunderstandings. And so we continued. This Facebook thing was becoming the other "F" word. All this nonsense was grape juice play in my mind. I felt like I was in a high school drama. I'm too mature for this, I thought to myself.

Yet other flirting was on planet Earth with food servers and the looks and attention he gave other wine when we were out. The red flags were starting to be more and more obvious. Some might find this healthy, innocent enough, and acceptable. It hit a nerve in me. I thought I was feeling hurt by this only because I had not experienced this in my life before, and perhaps because of the new experience, it was something I was unfamiliar with so, therefore, it made me feel uncomfortable. As time went by, my insecure feelings grew and I actually found myself retreating emotionally to self-protect. I allowed all the flirtatious behaviors to make me feel less than every other wine in the room and to negatively impact my self-esteem. I started losing the sexy feeling I had worked so hard to acquire. I was afraid I was going to become corked.

When I discussed my feelings with Max, he thought I was being insecure and assured me I had no reason to feel the way I did. He also tried to modify the behavior as best he could. Flirting was part of his personality. He was a natural. Asking him to change his personality to make me feel more secure, in my opinion, might be asking for too much. I did not want to flatten his personality, but I also did not want to be disrespected in front of other wine. He had me—a premium bottle of Cabernet—is there anything better? Perhaps he really likes to drink around, I thought.

Soon, I imagined he would cross the line in one of his flirtatious encounters and pop some other wines cork. The anxiety of worrying about how his personality would display itself toward other wine, and whether or not it would signal to them "open to blending," were my everyday thoughts. We discussed it plenty and concluded we had different value systems. Mine were a little too tight in his opinion and his were more decanted. Still I hung in there, trying to hold on to the good feelings I had, and enjoy the gifts I was receiving. There were plenty of them.

Max made love to me unselfishly, tried to please me, cook for me, fun and laughter filled our days at home, playing music, sharing a bubble bath and a glass of wine. He had an uncanny way he could feel my state of mind when we weren't together and texted me "Are you okay?" And there were the amazing insights he had in me that were shielded from my own awareness. Wow, he looked deep. And there were his poetic words that were piercing, that flowed out of him when he wanted to express an emotion and capture a moment. All our days were sexy, passionate, and fun. I never got tired of drinking him and each time I did, it felt like the first sip. But where he gave, he took.

Max had a way of keeping me on edge emotionally. Whether it was by constantly mentioning the characteristics he appreciated in other wine he dated before or knows—mostly in reference to their body, or some other characteristic of a movie star, singer, or athlete he was enamored with. Does it sound like more red flags? At first, I just dismissed the comments as insignificant tasting notes, but then the notes got louder and more frequent. I became annoyed and asked him to stop. He did.

I also asked him to stop flirting in public with other wine in front of me. He honored this request as well. He was good at "corrective action," he called it. "I can change my behavior to suit your needs." Even though he did not feel it was a big deal and thought I had made too much of it, he was happy to do anything for the sake of securing our blended status, and so I would feel safe again and go on experiencing my gifts. Then the cork would pop off in other ways—like the subtle undermines to jar my self-confidence in an attempt to make me feel inadequate. Like the times I shared memories about fun times I had with my business, in the past, and he commented: "Sounds good, but what have you done lately?" And other times, I would find him on dating sites checking out the labels and tasting notes of other wine. Definitely red flags! He also started a campaign to make me feel as though I had issues and was insecure when I questioned him about the behavior.

Max failed to identify the emotional pain it was causing and I started to retreat emotionally from our blend. I went back in the barrel. It was safe in there. I wasn't interested in dumping the wine and throwing the bottle away. I didn't want to give up. We blended well in other ways and it was worth the fight to me. I was trying to understand if this was just a case of a different varietal type that I was not accustomed to—after all, I was attracted to his charms and characteristics when I met him—now I was going to resent them? I guess I didn't like to share. I wanted the gift of him to be just for me without any risk of blending with others.

Max took me on a vacation and expressed all the ways he loved and appreciated me. He knew me well and had a good sense of who I was. He expressed great love for me and that he loved to look at me and could feel me in his heart and spirit. That our lovemaking was like nothing he had ever experienced and he thought I was a good person, intelligent and witty which he considered my charm. He said we fit together perfectly blended.

Max expressed a desire to have a half-bottle wine with me. I realized later this was a red flag of entrapment. Neither of us had any children. I had mourned in my divorce the loss of never having a child. It was surprising to me because I never wanted any children. The blend of Cab and I did not feel like the right blend to create a half bottle. My experience with Max awoke my suppressed desire. I imagined what it would be like to see a smaller version of this beautiful wine and the amazing smile that would delight me and bring joy to me. We saw a fertility doctor to explore our options. I even had an egg donor lined up if my eggs were not feasible. After all, I am a more mature wine. We tabled this option and worked on our blend.

Max conveyed to me that he wanted to work toward a long-term blend and marriage. He coaxed me out of the barrel. Once again, I felt secure and let down my guard to blend on all intimate levels—I completely decanted. I was determined to give this blend all I had to give, so I gave him all the love I had in the form of a place to hang out in my bottle, affection, acts of service, blending whenever he wanted, and all of my heart. We connected once again and our blend returned to the earlier experience, until one day, Max accompanied me to a meeting with an investor client of mine, who was also a close family friend.

I borrowed Max's laptop computer for my client presentation. As I exited PowerPoint to look something up on the internet, I found incoming emails from hookup dating sites. There Max was, with a picture of his bottle with tasting notes, and what he was looking for: "discreet affairs." Forget the red flags; I just got hit over the head with a wine bottle. My bottle cracked and all of me ended up in a puddle on the floor, flat and unable to breathe. I finished the presentation and looked at this beautiful wine seated across the table and thought, "Wow, this is the last time I will see him. Look how beautiful he is. I really did enjoy him. Why wasn't our blend enough for him? We've had the most amazing experiences together—the best times for me. He told me so many times our blend was what he always wanted and matched his wine vision board."

I confronted him that evening. It was New Year's Eve and we had a dinner to go to with my client and friend. So, I waited until we got back to the room where we were staying. He had no idea what was about to hit him over the head.

When I presented what I saw, Max became panicked, grasping to give me the explanation of being insecure with our blend after my confrontation with him over his online flirting. He thought I was going to dump him out and throw away his bottle, so he started a profile on various sites. He said he never blended with other wine on the sites, but occasionally, he liked to look at the "pretty wine bottles" and labels of other wine. He further shared that he needed the extra validation and used this avenue for attention. I did not understand why he had this need.

I decided to leave the blend. I conveyed to Max that I needed to focus on my business and have a blend break for a couple of months to heal from the emotional pain his behaviors were causing. I thought we might re-evaluate later. I started having health issues with my pituitary gland not functioning properly—a condition that occurred previously that I fought for years, now it was back. I read up on the condition, and found it is triggered by emotional pain. Imagine that. The emotional virus that entered me was causing my body not to work properly—just as a grape virus can compromise plant production in vines.

Initially, I was so confused. I thought I was the carrier of an emotional virus and had contaminated the blend. Perhaps I brought out the worst in the blend because I was relating with my old viruses, creating the same relational dysfunction over again. I was initially horrified I could be causing another person to be unstable in their life because I had underlying insecurities or jealousy issues. I wondered if this was divorce baggage I brought to the blend. I wondered if I was unhealed, and therefore, derailing my own attempt at happiness. I did years of counseling and spiritual work and waited until after my barrel refinement process. Why wasn't I ready for a healthy relationship?

IDENTIFYING THE ORIGIN OF EMOTIONAL VIRUSES

"A bottle of wine contains more philosophy than all the books in the world."

Louis Pasteur

I decided to take a long hard look at myself—again. I wondered if there were more viruses to be identified in my emotional make-up. I actually consulted with my mother over this; she was a member of a charismatic Christian church. The pastor was a spiritual healer and gifted in "prophetic word" which is looked upon as a message from divine inspiration or the Holy Spirit. I needed a message from God. I wanted someone to take a sample of my wine and place it under a microscope to determine if there was an emotional virus I was carrying compromising my ability to maintain a healthy blend. I needed a wine doctor. Please, I screamed inside, can someone look really closely and tell me what I have in me that could be ruining my life? I want to get rid of it; I want to be free from it. I'll do whatever it takes. More time in the barrel? No, please, not that again!

I was willing to do anything to have a chance at a healthy blend in the future and a chance at love. I asked my mother to arrange for me to meet with the Pastor of her church for a private tasting appointment after the service to receive prayer, spiritual healing, and any prophetic word that came to him. Maybe his finely tuned spiritual palate would detect the viruses in me. When I arrived, I had not yet been introduced to the pastor. The regular Sunday service was about to begin when low and behold, the Pastor opened the service with a prophetic word for me. He actually held up the service to deliver the message. Here is my prophetic word:

"The holy spirit is telling me there is a destiny in something happening between you and Max. Cheryl, you have a sense of seeing with eagle eyes with a quest to find reality and people you can trust. You are full of love and have angels around you. You are cautious to commit. You like to make sure God is in it. It is said to test all spirits to be of God. God is going to show you—words will pop off the page. You will have something to share of great value. You will discover with open eyes how people will be transformed by your wisdom. Your personality is a pillar. People will want to hear your wisdom. Spirits have been using people to hurt you. You have a destiny coming. God is bringing you to your destiny. Doors will open up. You will use what you have learned to help other people with a powerful voice. People will be transformed by your ministry. You know the destiny on you. You will open like a flower. Your counsel will help others that are wounded. You will be a powerful woman."

I was given this in a tape-recorded message after the service. I didn't understand its meaning or how it related to what I was experiencing until months later. I tucked my tape away, went back in the barrel and tried to make sense of my blend with Max.

I decided to meet with my mother for lunch later to get her opinion. It took a lot of courage for me to engage with her about my life. I did not trust her confidentiality. I had been let down before. My mother was on staff at the church and part of the ministry team. She clothed her bottle in Christianity. I learned from past experience not to be open or vulnerable with her. If I had a distress crack in my bottle, she seemed to find a way to break it completely whether intentional or not. Her critical nature, as far back as I can remember, was a constant source of emotional pain to me. While I did see some softening in her nature after becoming a Christian, I still felt her critical nature. I perceived, rightly or wrongly, that she had grown on a spiritual level, but her personality and emotional viruses were still intact; they had just been disguised better.

Interacting with my mother was a reminder of the absence of love I felt growing up. She didn't display any empathy. To put myself in her hands for some guidance was brave, especially with a fragile bottle. She could easily drop me on the floor without warning. I may not survive. I gave her a chance because she was trying to be a better person and I thought we could connect on a spiritual level. I believe we did connect to some degree, but she betrayed me in the end by sharing information about my life with other wine—I asked her to, once again, keep in confidence. My bottle didn't crack; I popped my cork, but it was close. She blew another chance at earning my trust, friendship, and a closer relationship with me. I had to distance myself again—just like I had been doing for the past fifteen years. I felt if she loved me, she should let me go to have a chance at a healthy life.

She was never there for me when I needed a mother for guidance or emotional support. She provided food, shelter, and clothes. By the time I was fourteen, I was starting to buy my own clothes and pay for my own incidentals with after-school jobs. I can recall something she said to me that changed the trajectory of my life experience; it set me up to carry a virus in my emotional make-up that contributed to hitting emotional and financial bankruptcy in my life. This virus was shielded from my awareness. But it was present in every relationship I ever had on any level. And so the story goes:

I was a teenager in great emotional despair over a boy. He was my first love in high school and one of my first opportunities for physical affection I craved. I do not remember ever being hugged as a child or told I was loved, and this young wine let me drink what I needed. When we relocated for my mother's job, he would visit me periodically. One day, I called his house and another wine answered (the head cheerleader) and told me she was blended with him and living with his parents because they were going to have a half bottle together. He never told me. He was still coming to see me. The devastation and shock was overwhelming. I cried in anguish. I thought I would not survive the blow. My bottle was about to crack. I couldn't face the world or go to school. I felt like I wanted to crack my own bottle and let the wine bleed out. I wanted to go to a hospital and get help, but I didn't want to ask my mother for anything. That might burden her and upset her which would lead to me having to take care of her feelings instead of mine.

To ask for something would be to risk being abandoned or punished, or the need would go unnoticed. That was a bigger pain I could not risk feeling. So, I learned to ask for nothing. This time wasn't any different than usual. I hoped, however, that I would send out enough distress signals my mother would notice, and for once, help me deal with the pain. She didn't notice, or if she did, she didn't do anything about it.

Since nothing was working to get her attention, I decided to take a lot of different pills at home to make myself obviously sick and in need of help. Some were her vitamins she took. Others were pain pills. I swallowed a concoction of pills hoping to get violently ill, and therefore, more obviously sick or in need of medical attention. When my mother came home from work, she saw the empty bottles. All I can remember her saying to me is "Did you take all those pills?" I replied, "Yes." Then she said, "Don't you cost me money to take you to the hospital." She never told me I was worthwhile or I would go on to experience a great life in the future or in any way support me with the pain and grief I was in. And so I got the message. It was loud and clear: "Do not cost others time or money or they will leave you." And so I didn't. Later that day, I got out the phone book and called the poison control center and told them what I took. They told me that taking vitamins and aspirin was not going to poison me, but might upset my stomach. I was about sixteen years old.

Most of my life growing up was about suppressing my needs and going unnoticed. This is how I coped with and learned to survive the dysfunction of my family environment. I have a memory for the conscious thought that I would not be responded to by my mother to get my needs met as early as age five or six. She was married at that time to my stepfather. I'm not sure what type of wine he was, but he was a real piece of work.

One day, I went to play in the sprinklers outside after school. I was in the first grade. I ran inside to get a towel, and water dripped on the floor. My stepfather thought that was unacceptable so he threw me on my bed, spit in my face, strapped a belt around me, and hung me up in a closet to dry. My mother was at the grocery store. I had this as a reoccurring dream, but I thought it was only a dream and never happened. The day I sought my mother's spiritual guidance she told me it was true. She had ordered him to take me down when she returned. She did not, however, enter the room to see what he had done, nor did she talk to me about it later.

He also made fun of me and watched me like a hawk. If I spilled a glass of milk at the dinner table, I got slapped. If I smiled and it exposed too many permanent teeth coming in, I was made fun of. It wasn't any wonder why I couldn't tape over or believe any compliments. I had carried around a negative self-image for years. How could I ever show weakness or need in this environment?

I have always been uncomfortable with receiving as far back as I can remember. I kept my independence and was happy to give more, and more, and more to others. But I rarely took. If I did that, others would take note and determine the cost of doing so was not worth having me around. And so, I also gave to my mother hoping she'd toss me an emotional bone one day.

I was also enslaved to my mother's illness when she was battling breast cancer. How could I walk away and have my own life when my mother was struggling for hers? I asked my boss at a furniture store to give me a promotion, so I could help support my family. I was promoted to an office manager at age nineteen. I supervised staff that was well into their fifties. I was, however, afraid of men at that age and I had a boss with a loud voice that sent me into the bathroom shaking at times. I even flinched once when I was in his office and he was letting off steam that had nothing to do with me. It was an emotional reflex. I've been running scared ever since—no one to fall back on, ever. I have to make it; I have no one to catch me if I fall.

I got an education; I worked my way up the corporate ladder. In my marriage blend, I allowed Cab to have the lifestyle he wanted and I took very little. I came to realize this deep rooted sense of unworthiness is ridiculous. I am so capable. I earned a great living. I am highly intelligent and skilled, but still I've never believed it, even after all I had accomplished in my careers and in my business. I dismissed every achievement, compliment, or praise. I never really heard them or believed. I had some narcissistic tendencies myself in that the compliments or achievements could never fill up the deep hole. I was needy. My emotional virus set me up to choose the partners I did. I became a caretaker in that I disconnected from my own needs and authentic self.

I lost my childhood growing up and became a parent in my teens (possibly sooner) to my mother's emotional, physical, and financial needs. I listened to her dating stories, took her to chemotherapy appointments, and waited in the lobby while she had numerous surgeries. I had no time to date or have any kind of life of my own. Long after she was healed from cancer, she still felt emotionally heavy on me. My two sisters from her marriage to my stepfather weren't getting what they needed. One of my sisters went to live with her dad. I used to bribe this sister to come over to visit me after I got my own apartment at age eighteen by buying her things I couldn't afford.

I received a call from her one day that indicated she might be getting some of the treatment I had received as a child from her dad and my stepfather. I wanted to save her from having to go through this, so I made a split decision to pay for a larger two-bedroom apartment and have her live with me. I was around twenty two and she was fourteen. I knew her dad wouldn't just let her go, so the two of us planned an escape. I sent her money through Western Union with a secret code. I arranged a taxi that took her to a bus that took her to the airport where a ticket was reserved for her to fly home. She lived with me for about a year and then went back to live with our mom. I had pleaded with my mom to take her back. I was strapped financially and I was trying to go to college. I had dropped my classes to be available to take my sister to and from her part time job. My mother asked me why she should take her back when after all "You're not doing anything with your life anyway." I was trying to, but cleaning up her messes was getting in my way. She wasn't my child and I didn't have this half bottle, she did.

After my sister went back to live with my mom, a few years later she became pregnant, got blended, and had a half bottle. After a few years blended, she divorced. She later had a hard time caring for her child on her own. She needed some family support. So, in another split decision that changed my life overnight, I went and picked up my niece and she lived with me for about a year. I had just started a new position and was dating my first boyfriend since high school—I was twenty-five years old.

My boyfriend took a job oversees as an architect and after my niece was reunited with her mom, I met Cab at the financial services company where I took my new position as a bookkeeper for the tax department. After Cab and I were blended, after a three year tasting period, I went back to school and finished my degree. I tried to distance myself as much as possible from my mother, so I could live my own life. I couldn't stand to be in her presence and hear any negative remarks. She had a critical nature that would find fault in my hair, make-up, face, clothes I was wearing, it didn't matter. It felt like a razorblade slashing my label.

It would take days to glue my emotional label back together. I was defensive around her and it would seem rude to outsiders, but it was a defensive strategy to beat her back before she had a chance to attack my self-esteem. One thing though, she could never attack my character. I was a Cabernet with good character. I tried to do the right thing, always.

As my marriage started dying on a vine, Cab complained that I treated him like my mother—with the same defensive armor. As time went by, more and more, he reminded me of my mother. His selfishness in our blend was similar, and the sarcasm he spewed at me slashed my label in the same manner. Just as my mother had not returned the love I hoped to win through my devotion and care, I never got what I wanted or needed from my marriage. In both cases, I think it was unattainable. It was like a bottle of Abacus dangling in my face, but I couldn't drink it. I could only hope one day I could have an opportunity to taste what I had been dreaming and hoping for—love in a wine glass. Instead, every time I got close enough to it to smell its bouquet, the glass moved farther and farther away, just out of reach, but within my line of vision. I couldn't earn a taste either. I gave and gave and gave, but I wasn't worthy to drink the nectar of the Gods; that was for the worthy people. I got my pseudo love in other ways: through success and celebrating with my purchased bottle of Abacus and other fine wines. Turns out, you can buy this stuff for yourself; no one has to give it to you.

I don't believe we are put on earth to sacrifice our lives to be enslaved to others. If I do not value myself properly, how can I expect others to? My lack of boundaries let others take more than what is healthy and mutually beneficial. I can attract users or needy people who want me to serve them. They can spot me as though I have a tasting note on my label that says "Use me. I am unworthy."

I just have to watch where I give too much. I am not motivated by money either. I like the emotional deposit of a job well done. A recognition that I helped make a difference with a sense of purpose or satisfaction. I have learned to expect to be paid for my time. I need money to live.

My mother did send me a letter, which is the most human response I have ever received from her in my entire life. Perhaps there are some feelings in her somewhere. I've really never seen them before. Here is my letter:

Hi Cheryl,

I realized after I heard Dr. Drew this week how suppressed emotions can affect you later in life. And that's what you may have, suppressed emotions. I'm sorry I didn't know better when you were growing up... and I'd like to know if you can forgive me. I do know now that I've always loved you and wanted good things for you. Suppressed emotions are what caused my anxiety and nervousness. It came out in my health years later. It wasn't until I fully let God come into my heart and his Holy Spirit filled me with his love that I could feel and know that kind of love and show it to other people. I'm truly sorry for what I was unable to give you back then. I was trying to make you happy by dressing you good and buying things to play with....I didn't know any better, but I do now! I thought that was what you do. I would like another chance for us to be friends and enjoy each other's company. I do enjoy being around you. I want things to be different for you. And to show you I do love you and care about your life. If there's anything that I can help you with I will be there for you. You have a good heart and a lot of compassion. You are a very caring person and have always been there for your family. I could always trust you and depend on you. You always kept your word. And still a very good person...You look very good and with your hair long and you being thin...you're young for your age... you will look good for a very long time. You are beautiful inside and out!You never really got to know me like you should of. I should have opened up more—instead of just doing things. I'm sorry for that. I'm still praying for you. And I hope you had a nice birthday...and with people you enjoy being around.

I'll always be your mother and Love you, Momma

THE VIRUS CONTAMINATED MY BLEND

"I am not sure I trust you. You can trust me with your life,
My King. But not with my wine, obviously. Give it back."

Megan Whalen Turner, *The King of Attolia*

After revisiting some of the wounds of my childhood that
contributed to my emotional viruses, I turned my attention to
Max. I got curious one day to go online and see if I could find
some of Max's behaviors and how others perceived them. This
is when I found him. "Seek and ye shall find" and what I came
to feel as the truth set me free. I found the behaviors prevalent
and the emotional dynamic of our blend in article after article. It
was like someone had written our story after witnessing all our
private events. It is my opinion that Max suffers from a personality
disorder called Borderline Personality Disorder (BPD). It was
undeniable. I had lived with it firsthand. I really wasn't cracked
after all I thought.

This was the first time I had heard of BPD. Finally, after all
the confusion and heartache, I could see with great clarity.
No surprise it was difficult to see. This was well before I had
my rose-colored glasses prescription changed to wine-colored
glasses. Maybe I didn't want to see. I just wanted him to love
me.

This propelled me to spend hours upon hours reading books,
journals, and BPD sites. Everything I read about BPD pointed to
infancy and childhood abandonment trauma as the leading cause.
This trauma results from inadequate bonding and emotional
closeness with a child's mother or primary caregiver and can also
result from traumatic emotional, physical, or sexual abuse.

This original core wound of abandonment develops into "splitting" which is a defense mechanism that borderlines will act out when they feel emotions today that resemble the feelings of their original core wound. They, in essence, have a black and white way of relating. The Borderline split is "get away—come closer" and "I hate you—don't leave me." Max would pull me close to him emotionally and then sabotage that closeness with his distancing behaviors to push me away when he felt he could be at risk for abandonment.

Perceived abandonment could be imagined or real and over the slightest behavior I exhibited. He could read abandonment in me becoming too successful, physically fit, or secure in myself. He perhaps thought it was a matter of time before his worst fears were a reality and I moved on to blend with another wine. Yet, I had all I wanted in front of me. George Clooney could have knocked on the door with his big glass of Abacus and I would have told him I was busy—busy drinking this amazing Riesling and loving every minute of it.

I further read that a person who suffers from BPD will go to great lengths to get their needs met. And because their needs are a deep hole of unmet needs and deep childhood wounds, they have become seductive and coy in their approach to getting what they want. On the outside, they can capture your attention with their well-packaged delivery. This bottle stands out on the shelf when you are shopping for wine with its beautiful label. In many cases, they have a charismatic and charming personality and are the life of the party. This is part of the over compensation for what they know: that they have deep flaws emotionally, so this outward persona is camouflage. They take pride in their appearance, might even sport an athletic bottle.

They want to connect emotionally because they need it. Their psyche is so shattered they have lost a sense of themselves and feel empty most of the time. When the original core wounds occurred, they were not developed enough emotionally to deal with the trauma; therefore, the abuse created a discord in their emotional development. They are not fully integrated emotionally; the transmission of their psyche can slip in a moment's notice. They suffer from emotional deregulation. Healing for them would require integrating the wounds into their psyche to re-process the wounds in a healthy way now that they are more developed to deal with and heal from the trauma. It's not as easy as it sounds.

When children are wounded at a very young age, they don't even have the concept of language to process traumatic events. All they can feel is the terror imposed upon them and the pain that is so great their underdeveloped psyche shatters before they have a chance to develop healthy emotional regulation from a nurturing and loving caregiver.

They develop boundary issues with others because people have crossed healthy boundaries with them. They lack impulse control, and often times cross boundaries in a business or social setting. They lack the containment of skin, so to speak. Their juice can run out before they realize they are leaking. It's no wonder they are finding the next bottle to host them. Their first words in an encounter should be "Please, I need a home. Is there room for two in your bottle?" The problem with sharing your bottle is you have to pour some of you out before you can let someone else in. At first, it feels cozy and warm, snuggled up and nourishing to have some other wine to drink other than your own. Slowly but surely though, you will lose a little more of your wine over time; slight movements in the bottle will inadvertently dump out part of you until you can't find any of you left. You might think you can afford to lose a little bit of yourself. The experience is intoxicating. After all, you've been drinking a lot. You don't know you're dying slowly because you're drunk. Love drunk.

This wine is the most seductive wine, with the prettiest label and most intoxicating bouquet. One taste of this stuff and it will blow your palate. One taste will not be enough; you will be hooked by the first sip. You'll drink them up so fast you'll be intoxicated before the alcohol level reaches your bloodstream. As a matter of fact, you might feel drunk just being around them without taking the first sip—as I did. But it won't be everything it's cracked up to be.

Red flags will be quickly dismissed because nothing can get you to relinquish this bottle once you have it in your hands. You will want to hold on tight and not share it with anyone. This special bottle is the sublime nectar of the Gods and you found it. If you share it, no one would return it and it would slip from your hands forever. After you taste this wine, it will set a new standard and you will wonder if you could ever drink anything else again. The taste as it hits your palate is a life altering experience. It brings you to life somehow and has super powers to bring bright colors to your world and euphoria that you have only read about in cheap romance novels, totally unattainable—until now!

What do you do with this bottle of wine? You take it home—what else? And that is exactly what I did. Do you blame me? Wouldn't you have done the same?

When I met Max, I had never heard of Borderline Personality Disorder (BPD). I didn't know what to watch for in the form of red flags. I don't know if it would have mattered if I had heard of the disorder. It would not have changed the initial connection. There was no warning sign on the label to say "Danger, drinking this could be hazardous to your health." Quite the contrary, the label made fabulous promises. Some of them were delivered; some were not. "Hang on" is all I can say when choosing this bottle—it's going to be a volatile journey.

Isn't everyone deserving of a life of love and happiness? Especially wounded souls with BPD who have suffered at the hands of their caregivers or others they relied on to love and care for them to meet their developmental needs. Instead, they were betrayed. And now, it's even harder for them to get what they need consistently.

Looking back, I realized I overlooked the red flags early on in the initial contact and failed to take notice or dismissed them. It was my choice. You can always find these red flags if you watch, wait, and observe. In my case, I must have thought to myself "Lie to me, baby" and I'll let you. Just let me taste the sublime nectar of your delicious wine. Sounds like the lyrics from yet an all-too-familiar tune. I guess this is nothing new. What makes me so special? The truth be known, I was the kind of wine that blended perfectly with him, and that made me special. He chose me for my emotional make-up as much as I chose him. We chose each other—there wasn't even a decision to be made; it happened without thought in our initial encounter.

As time went by, Max would subtly undermine my sense of self-worth with defeating comments aimed at hitting my weakest insecurities—like the sense of unworthiness I carried around since childhood, my biggest wound. He collected other ones as well that he learned by getting close to me. I believe this was on a subconscious level programmed by his emotional virus. The authentic Max—when the virus wasn't controlling him under his emotional wiring—was a tender loving and kind soul. When he looked inside me, he might have been collecting information, but he also identified the authentic wine I am and acknowledged me at my purest form. He found parts in me that were hidden and drew them out and presented them to me. He praised me with one hand, and tore me down with the other.

Our lovemaking was very sensual, sweet, passionate and playful. There weren't any parts of Max that were neglected. If he were wine spilled on the floor, I licked up every drop and wasted nothing. He gave back and then some, always pleasing me before himself. With Max, I felt the most beautiful I have ever felt in my life and the ugliest at the same time from his distancing behaviors. Everything about this relationship had two extreme polar opposites and I was just trying to stay on the positive side.

Herein lies the problem: you can't have one side without the other with BPD. The good comes with the bad. And you'll never know which one you are going to get from one moment to the next. It can change before you have a chance to swallow a sip of wine. From one moment, you will be looked at with great adoration, and the next, you will be dismissed as insignificant as they fail to take ownership of the emotional pain they cause. In hindsight, I realize the confusion, anxiety, and instability in the emotional integrity of the relationship started hitting up against my childhood wounds. One by one the scabs were coming off and I started bleeding emotionally from my unresolved childhood wounds, the ones I wasn't aware I was carrying around in the form of emotional viruses.

I was on the other side of Max's personality and the perfect host. I had adopted a dysfunctional adaptation of caregiving and willingness to forego my needs and put other people's before my own. This is how I learned to survive growing up with my mother and stepfather during the years they were blended. I felt undeserving of emotional support or empathy from another because it was absent when I grew up. The compromised emotional make-up of Max did not offer a healthy exchange of emotional currency. I allowed him to pay less and make withdrawals with his distancing behaviors, subtle undermines, and lack of empathy when I expressed hurt feelings. I accepted, to some degree, what he had to offer because of my perceived value: the value I was given by my mother, my biological father, and my step-father. I felt undeserving, so I was willing to take less than what I deserved—just as I was willing to eat the leftovers from boy's night out in my marriage. I thought I was done taking the scraps.

When I decided to start dating after my divorce, I vowed to choose someone who was emotionally available, athletic, liked to cook, spontaneous, fun, passionate, and would appreciate me with words of affirmation and acts of service. Be careful what you wish for. I did get exactly what I wanted. I took what Madonna refers to in her song as "a chance on a beautiful stranger." I didn't hesitate when the tasting notes I desired were matching the taste I was having. He was open on an emotional level; we connected deeply. I opened up like never before and all of me that was hiding for so long came out to play. The authentic re-produced wine comfortable in her own skin came out to live and play and not afraid to be herself. I felt confident and sexy. He was the perfect canvas to paint an expression of me. I liked being myself with him. It made me wonder how life might have been different if I would have had more love in my life. He nurtured me after the emotional bankruptcy in my life; he was like pure nourishment—as though I was brought back to life by CPR (cataclysmic, passionate, rescue). Emotional intimacy combined with passionate lovemaking and I was transported to another world far, far away from the one I had been living in. He seemed to adore me, maybe even love me, I thought.

We spent quality time playing together, listening to music, laughing, taking bubble baths, and giving each other coconut oil massages, and staying naked on Sundays. There wasn't anything I didn't like doing with Max. I loved being with him, looking at him, touching him, smelling him, sleeping spooned with him. If it weren't for the distancing behaviors, I would have married him in a heartbeat. I cherished every moment. I didn't want it to end.

When I looked at Max, he became a mirror that I could see my reflection in. He felt familiar, like the other half of me—probably because there was no escaping him with the two of us living in the same bottle. By loving him, it was like loving me. I saw my broken parts in him reflecting back at me. I had wounds too.

I couldn't drink enough of Max. Oh please, just one more sip, please another, and another. Now that I've tasted the wine I had always hoped to drink, I don't want to let it go. Cabernet Sauvignon? Forget that stuff. Pour it out. This Riesling is unbelievable. No longer a Cabernet snob, this wine opened ready to drink, had the most intoxicating bouquet, the length was long as it lingered in my mouth, and the finish, sweet and silky, with an intriguing essence of something I didn't recognize, but it worked well with the overall experience. I gave him all of me. I surrendered my heart, soul, mind, and bottle. I wanted to love him with everything I had. I felt he deserved it. He was worthy. I didn't hold anything back. I loved bigger than I ever had before. I was willing to gamble for love and risk everything to keep drinking this wine. I was addicted.

I turned into a wino and my wine of choice was Max. I surrendered my bottle, label, cork, and all the liquid in me. I can't resist this wine. I've now experienced a cataclysmic collide that blended Max with me and me with him. It felt good to be loved in an all-consuming way. I drank him up. I marveled at his charismatic personality. His fun loving ways delighted me every day. I really didn't even need to drink him. He had me at the smell of his bouquet.

Imagine a blend like this to be met with abrupt distancing techniques—what happened to this wine? It was open a minute ago! Once stressed or triggered, a borderline's defense mechanism will distance you after you've enjoyed a time of closeness or over a sense of or perceived abandonment threat. This defense originates from the original core wound of abandonment in childhood. A borderline will treat you as if you are the wine with whom they experienced the abandonment. It's no longer about you. It's about the person who wounded and terrorized them to begin with.

It's about the person who didn't give them what they needed. Who is this person? Is it a bad mother? Or, a mother who made bad choices and didn't know how to properly care for a child? Perhaps a mother who was, herself, wounded from her own childhood. Oh God, I cry for the pain the neglectors and abusers have caused people with BPD. This beautiful Riesling I love is living with deep emotional pain. I've further read that Borderlines feel empty and a loss of self. They have been robbed of their rightful emotional development of a human being. Animals do better to care for their young. I imagine this beautiful baby boy smiling with his beautiful smile as he gazes up at his mother in great need "Here I am, mommy. Do you see me? Do you love me mommy? I love you."

I'd like to ask his mother a few questions. Didn't you see the gift in front of you and that he needed you? Did you see those amazingly beautiful eyes and a smile that never held back? He was worthy. He did not ask to be born. He had a life to live with healthy emotional capacity to enjoy. Were you the one that took this away? I'll be his mom. I love him like you never did. I'll look at him and appreciate him. I'll tell him he is beautiful, appreciated, and worthwhile. I'll tell him he is the best thing that happened to me. I'll thank God for him.

It must have been you that abandoned him by not meeting his emotional development needs. What else did you do to him? Did you abuse him physically or sexually? You left him screaming inside with pain. So much pain it was too much to handle, so he split off to save himself from what was too painful. This permanently damaged his emotional regulation. He wasn't old enough to meet his own needs through other people. You were supposed to give him what he needed. Why weren't you there for him? Why did you choose to hurt your child? I have no compassion for you. Are you going to take responsibility or see the error of your ways? You made the choice to neglect.

There are laws that that protect children from physical and sexual abuse and neglect. Emotional abuse should be a crime too. Too bad it's too hard to see until the damage has been done. Maybe children should have the right to press charges later, after they are aware of the limitations imposed upon them through physical, emotional, and sexual abuse. Sometimes victims become the abusers. At some point, the cycle has to end. Someone has to take responsibility and learn to do better.

I'd like to ask the one who neglected or abused him if they know this empty place they've put him in. I try to imagine what this feels like. Maybe I've been there in that numbness of grief and time in the barrel when I didn't have a sense of who I was while I was re-producing. But this was temporary. BPD is every day for the rest of your life. I think of him having to carry the emotional wounds around not feeling whole, satisfied, and without the terror of you—the neglector and abuser who failed to give him what he needed and hurt him so much he broke. I hate you for what you did. Then you punished him when he was growing up for his rage. He was a bad boy, he acted out. You created him and you are brutalizing him again. You can't take it back now. The damage is already done. All he can do is manage the best he can through on-going therapy. You cheated him out of a life he could have had. You didn't do your job and he has to pay the price. Where is your punishment? You should be in jail.

I'll heal you, Max. I'll love you enough. I won't leave you. I have childhood wounds too. My father wasn't there. I never felt loved. My deep feelings of unworthiness mirror you. Maybe together we can make a whole bottle of wine—two half bottles to make a whole. Yet, I am just a wine, not God, not a therapist, not even a mom. I can't take you pushing me away after I get close to you. Please forgive me if I am like the one who left you. I have too much emotional pain as a result of your defense mechanisms.

Not all Borderlines are alike. Many are narcissistic—they like attention. They can be extremely jealous, lie, have poor impulse control, and extramarital affairs, often self-harming behaviors, suicidal ideation, stalking, low self-esteem, irrational abandonment fears, and a lack of empathy. It was all coming together. He used the internet to feed his narcissistic needs for attention and maybe to hook up for sex. He could not control his flirting and often had what I perceived as a lack of healthy boundaries with other wine whether in a social or professional situation. All of his erratic emotions and behaviors were camouflaged under divorce rubble. I thought for most of the time the behaviors were situational to the set of circumstances and struggles we were in to rebuild our lives. It became evident he wasn't coming out of the cycle and we were not rebuilding as we should be. We were surviving, but we were not thriving. The emotional chaos was causing instability in our financial recovery and setting back my barrel refinement process. I had to let Max go for him and for me. I did not want him to spend time on our blend anymore. I wanted him to concentrate on himself.

He tried so hard to monitor his behavior and control his impulses. He was using his will to overcome his emotional virus. I appreciated his tremendous effort. It is not sustainable. The will is not strong enough. I decided I wanted Max to take care of Max and not worry about taking care of me. My feelings of unworthiness surfaced again from childhood and I left him not because I found out he suffers from BPD (I figured this out after I left), but because I am a wine that hurts when the wine I love gives attention to other wine online or by way of flirting in my presence. I did not feel I could trust him. As part of his control, all the emotional deposits he made by placing me on the top shelf were overdrawn by keeping me emotionally unstable and in fear of losing him, a set of abandonment issues on my end to keep me living in fear.

What? There is no cure? No pill to take? There is only therapy for a lifetime to help manage the disorder better? I wanted to help fix Max. Can I put him in a barrel and re-produce him? Max is broken emotionally. Can't a therapist put him back together? Can't I love him enough to make up for all the wounds he has inside and heal him? No, of course not, only God can do that. These wounds don't heal like physical wounds where you just have to be patient and let the body heal itself. Borderlines get to carry these emotional wounds around with them forever. They are never able to rid themselves of the trauma of the past. It's there day after day distorting their emotions and leading them to continually self-sabotage all attempts of a healthy, loving relationship.

The day I found Max's behaviors online I cried that day like never before. Not for me, but for Max. It didn't end here though; I still had a desire for more understanding. I was fascinated, but mostly I was looking for a treatment, a pill, or a fix. Someone must have been cured somehow, I thought.

I also thought to myself how fortunate I was to have my grandmother take care of me while my mother worked. She must have met my needs. Otherwise, without her, I may have been at risk to develop a personality disorder. I'm not sure I would have been as fortunate if my mother was my sole caregiver. I never felt an emotional bond with my mother. Thank you, Grandma Gladys, for my life.

You see, Max connected all the dots in my life. My absentee father, and emotionally unavailable mother, my marriage blend, and others I allowed myself to be enslaved to in my life in hopes of one day receiving the love I'd earn through giving. Never believing that I was worthy without working myself to death. Little did I know you should be loved with no strings attached and appreciated for the wine you are. Love is the nurturing ingredient in winemaking. It's the emotional part filled with passion. The science of winemaking will always be there. But the love comes from pure appreciation for the wine that pours into your glass and the experience you have when drinking it. I never felt good enough just to show up in someone's glass. I was conditioned to serve.

My life experience set me up to be emotionally needy after years of neglect. Colliding with Max was like finding an oasis of nourishment emotionally and physically. Yes, it took a borderline to bring me back to life. Max awakened all the emotions I had suppressed since childhood. The intense feelings I felt were in me! He broke through barriers until he exposed all my hidden parts. He is responsible for me being able to experience myself in complete wholeness. I found the person I could be and was capable of being. Not the broken down, beat down version, but the real me under all my protective armor, bottle, and labels. After divorce, I didn't know if I could come back to feel so strongly for another. I never knew the wine I was with Max. The new and improved wine was someone I experienced for the first time.

Max let me see his wounds too. He talked to me about his childhood wounds. Originally, I thought he was wounded by divorce much like I thought I was. Looking at him was like seeing my reflection in a mirror. When I loved him it was as though I loved myself—maybe even healed myself. I gave him what I always wanted: words of affirmation, acts of service, and a kind and affectionate touch. I loved to nurture his spirit and give him praise and admiration for the qualities I enjoyed in him. I did not hold back. He was a beautiful person. He liked helping people. He was fun loving and attentive and thoughtful to look after me. Did I mention I loved to smell him? His smile took my breath. He had the most beautiful face and body. I tried hard to be worthy of my gift. I worked constantly to be as desirable as I could and I thanked God every day for Max.

MAY I HAVE MY WINE BACK PLEASE?

"There is a smile of love, and there is a smile of deceit, and there is a smile of smiles in which these two smiles meet."

William Blake

Max is gone now. He is no longer there to keep my bottle warm at night nor delight me with his presence. This Riesling wine evaporated into thin air. It was there a moment ago and now I can't even find evidence of its existence. Not even a lingering hint of the bouquet. Maybe I imagined the whole thing. Either that or the joke's on me. I can, however, feel the essence of his spirit, and the absence of it has left a dull ache inside me. I worked so hard to stay blended and perhaps he did too. I even dumped part of me out of my bottle to make room for him. Now, I'm wondering how I get my wine back. I know! I'll go back into the barrel and add some extra yeast to my wine and double my volume. Maybe I can fake being a full bottle of wine for a while. I won't let anyone taste me, so they won't know the difference. This kind of emptiness must feel like that daily gray area, the void and emptiness I've read BPDs suffer and that makes me even sadder to think about.

I met with him a few months after I left him at a beautiful resort hotel along the beach. I wanted to share my interpretation. Was I right? I wondered. It was a sunny day. We could be a regular couple out for the day enjoying each other's company. I'd like to think, in at least some small way, I left him with something. Good memories he credits me for he says, So many amazing times." He still tells me "I love you" and he apologizes for the emotional impact of his behaviors.

We drank coffee and I gave him the research material I had collected and studied about Borderline Personality Disorder. I wanted to know if this was his emotional virus. If so, my hope was that he would enter therapy and gain control over some of the distancing behaviors. You don't want to waste time letting a disorder control you, I said to him. He didn't answer but took the research material I had collected. If he knew, I'm glad he didn't share this with me when we met. I would have looked up BPD on the internet and been scared to enter into the blend, afraid I would end up getting hurt. If I never had entered into this blend, I wouldn't have connected the dots in my life and opened up my unhealed wounds to look at them and work on healing them or managing them better. I also tasted the best wine I ever had and hope I can hit the tasting notes again with a new blend.

I don't want to paint too pretty of a picture—don't want to start a "hook-up with a Borderline" website with the tag line "Get in touch with your true self." This was an experience that helped me; I grew from it. But it didn't come without great pain. I caution anyone with a newly healed heart coming out of a divorce to smack their bottle against a wall with anyone who doesn't have control over their emotional viruses. Watch out for the red flags. My understanding from reading some literature written by mental health professionals is there is a concentration of BPDs on online hook-up sites—used mainly for casual sex, not to mention, mainstream dating sites for wine looking for exclusive blends. It makes sense to me. Many have increased cravings for physical touch and sex and many suffer from an inability to control their impulses. BPD affects each person somewhat differently. With all the relationship fall-out this disorder causes, hooking up to get basic needs met without any strings attached seems like the perfect forum for a Borderline. Apparently, some Borderlines don't seek therapy until their looks are gone. Their captivating charm feeds their narcissism. I imagined Max out hooking up with beautiful women—my biggest fear while in the blend. Now, there are no blend boundaries to get in the way of Max acting on his impulses.

Sometimes I ask myself if this experience was worth it. When I first left Max, I was angry. I must have played the artist Adele's "Rolling in the Deep" twenty times a day. I could relate to her lyrics of being deceived. Sound familiar to anyone? I was beat down emotionally from the distancing techniques that were designed to keep me on edge and off-kilter. He repeatedly hurt my feelings by trying to make me feel inadequate compared to other wine. I felt I was going insane at times, trying to explain how the comments were affecting me and causing anxiety. "Get over it," I was told. "Move on." I guess that was easy for him to say.

I may never know if I am right about Max and BPD but my anger has left and turned to sadness and compassion. If I am right, BPD has also taken some of the good experiences with it. Perhaps they were not always genuine or real, but layered with manipulation and deceit. The truth is they were real to me, so I get to keep the experience of what I felt. My feelings were real. My actions conveyed my true feelings. I loved me blended with Max. I liked the notes I hit. In a way, I took my new wine out after I was released from the barrel for a tasting appointment. I liked her; she was fun, passionate, sexy, witty, and capable of loving someone. She was alive and parts of her that weren't for most of her life came to the surface. Max helped me experience all of me. He showed me my hidden parts that were out of my line of vision. He did not make me what I became; he participated in me being me.

With some therapy, I hope Max enters into, I believe he will be able to manage the disorder better and have an even better blend in the future. I'm a little envious of who will get to drink this new wine after his barrel refinement process. But then I think to myself, he was the perfect wine for me, just what I needed, and I enjoyed every drop.

I read this letter to Max to describe my experience:

Max,

You delighted me with your boyish charm, playfulness, physical beauty, and spirit. I could lie next to you for a lifetime just to smell your bouquet. I felt happy just waking up next to you and seeing your face as you smiled at me. I felt grateful to be alive more than any other time in my life. When you distanced yourself, I missed you. I waited for you to show up again with the gifts you gave.

Thank you for your gifts. There were so many. I felt love through your actions when you took care of me in all your special ways. My time with you will forever be bittersweet. But I have no doubt you were just what I needed. You were meant to teach me more about myself and to reconnect me to who I can be and how I can feel. I believe you were my destiny. You opened up my emotional wounds and showed me places that were not yet healed, not from my divorce, but from my childhood. I finally received the lesson and understanding of my life to evolve to a higher awareness level. I am forever grateful for the gift of you and the lessons learned.

I love your spirit. You have a sweet soul. I felt you. We were close and we were connected for a very long time after we were no longer physically together. Sending me text messages from out of the blue in response to my internal thoughts of you were uncanny. I had a very hard time letting you go. I have learned to be at peace.

You did not deserve what was done to you as a child. I tried to love you enough to fix it and to put you at ease to know I would be there to love you as long as you wanted me to. Remember when I would look at you for a long time without looking away and smile? That was one way I was trying to tell you I loved you and that I wasn't afraid to be vulnerable and risk it all to be close to you. I'll always remember your smiling face and the way you stroked my forehead before sleep saying: "Pretty girl, pretty girl." The negative comments and feelings of unworthiness I carried inside me would melt away with each stroke from the warmth of your touch. I loved sleeping intertwined with you, safe and warm.

Thank you for showing me all my parts. Broken, alive, buried. I've got a much better picture of who I am. I've grown so much. You might not recognize me now. Thank you for spending the time we had together. I was always so proud to be by your side. I wanted you. I tried to keep you bottled up with me with the cork on tight. But I knew I had to let you go. Our destiny had been fulfilled. I could not contain you any longer.

May you find love and happiness and live a beautiful life that you deserve.

Love, Cheryl

MAY I HAVE MY WINE BACK PLEASE?

I found a business card I had on-hand from several years prior amongst some papers during one of my moves. I realized Max was the blonde German man I had met briefly in business when I returned from a European vacation. The same one I had the thought "Wow what a beautiful sweet German wine. Who is the lucky lady who gets to drink him?" Well, he was delicious.

LET THE WINE POUR

"I tasted – carless – then – I did not know the wine came once a world – Did you? Oh, had you told me so – This thirst would blister – easier – now"

Emily Dickinson

Sometimes love is not meant to stay, but to flow through you like a current to recharge you and bring renewed passion and wonder to your life. To hold on to it would be to stifle its energy that is meant to flow freely into the river of life. Water left to pond only turns murky and undrinkable.

Fairy tales are not books, but chapters in life. You turn the page and write a new story. Interconnected experiences culminate the book of life. Two souls colliding to dance, intertwine with, and refine the soul with new perspective and emotion. Two broken souls that fit perfectly together like a jigsaw puzzle—perfect pieces to heal, to hurt, and to evolve. It starts with a look, a touch, openness. The bond that develops is a twist of fate and a serendipitous microcosmic chance...or is it?

Do you know the same souls over and over again in multiple lifetimes? I do not know. Do you wander the earth in search of your friend with your psychic energy moving you through this time and space, longing to connect and feel their presence? Maybe it is a combination of new people you meet and old souls that reconnect to provide you with the lessons to help you evolve.

I knew Max wasn't meant to stay. I knew his brokenness was delivered to me in exactly the perfect form to match my brokenness. He was perfect just the way he was. Perhaps there are reasons love could not be sustained, but for a moment, the experience was so intense it woke up every cell in my body that now stands in attention. I am forever changed.

I wanted to know if it really happened. Was it real between us? And then it dawned on me, of course it was—the experience changed me. I was able to release the pain and embrace the ever-lasting gift. Sometimes from pain we are given our greatest gifts. Out of pain, we grow. I had the gift of understanding. Now, I had the power of awareness to change the direction of my life.

Sure, maybe I was healed from divorce, but I was not healed from or aware of the childhood emotional viruses that were alive in me. The price to pay for this lesson was worth it. This quest to win love enslaved me on a never-ending journey that leads to nowhere. At some point, the exhaustion catches up. You've got nothing left in you to keep going—emotional bankruptcy. Take the lesson in love and loss and move on. Your soul evolved, and in order to continue to grow, we need new experiences—some happy and some painful.

I have nothing more to wine about. The place in my bottle that was once reserved for Max has now been filled with the pages of this book. Look inside my bottle at my wine and see that it has great clarity, there is nothing hiding—an open book. I spent the next year earning my divorce coach certification and writing. I decided to move from the Orange County coast to the coast of Los Angeles for a new release. I've made some new wine friends. I'm looking forward to starting a new chapter.

WINE MAKES THE WORLD GO AROUND

"Where there is no wine there is no love."

Euripides

At the end of the day, I've learned we are all really a blend of different wines. No matter what kind of wine we think we are. Our tasting notes change at different times in our life. At times, we are spicy; sometimes we are bold; sometimes a little fruity; and sometimes the Pinot Noir in us will show up when we least expect it; other times, the Riesling. Some of us have cracked bottles we hide under pretty labels. Sometimes we pop our corks, and sometimes we become corked. Some of us have picked up sediments along the way. Some wine never matures. Sometimes we don't store ourselves properly and aren't authentic on our labels. Other times, we try to pass ourselves off as a wine we are not. Next time you judge a wine too harshly for its taste, you might remind yourself that you hit some bad notes, too, in your lifetime.

We can learn something from any wine. We are mirrors reflecting back at each other through our shiny bottles. Rarely do our bottles completely camouflage what is inside. You've got to join the wine club of life—sharing yourself with others while tasting other wine. Each drink adds another varietal to your blend. Sometimes we will be spit out and sometimes we will be the ones to spit others out. Sometimes we have to spend time drinking our own wine to become reacquainted with and appreciate the wine we are.

Drink up, Buttercup. Variety is the spice of life. You've got to get stomped on as a grape to get your juice out. You need to spend time in the barrel to build character and maturity, and upon release, you are a premium wine, rich with life experience. You'll be appreciated by those who drink you. We have to look at the stomping we get in life as a chance to learn and refine our perspective.

We've got to love all the varietals in us, unconditionally, and make allowances for the notes we are not up to delivering. We may hit them when we are ready. Our values will give us our character. Our courage will decant us. Our time in the barrel will mature us. Our experience will give us complexity. We've got to make the best of our life experience, lessons, and times we get to go back in the barrel. We've got to grieve to love again, and have the courage to take the chance to decant fully with all the vulnerability, so we can taste the sublime nectar of life.

Our bottles may break; our hearts may break. We may get stripped of our labels and become a shiner. We may even lose everything we've ever known. If we are lucky, we won't lose our humanity or our ability to desire more. Don't hide out in the barrel, there's a life waiting that is uniquely yours. All your pain and sorrow will give you the ability to relate, tolerate, and understand. If we do not understand, we will get another lesson in the future. We will continue to grow and mature over time. Sadness will eventually turn to joy and happiness. Open your heart, learn to forgive, and recognize it is impossible to be perfect—although some wine comes pretty close. Some of us are perfect in our brokenness for our life purpose.

So, in the end, what kind of wine do you want to become?

A Meritage!

ACKNOWLEDGEMENTS

I wish to thank my dearest friend Emily who not only shared many years of my childhood with me, she has consistently been there to support me and believe in me through my divorce journey and beyond. I love you and thank you for your friendship. You are family. Your wisdom strengthens me. Thank you for lifting the lid on my barrel and making sure I was still in there. I wish to thank Tom who called me to check on me even if it was to talk "wine babble," I appreciate it. I wish to thank Iris for her intuitive insights and readings. I wish to thank Michael who gave me a piece of wisdom that strengthened my spirit. I wish to thank Victoria who was my best wine-drinking budding during divorce. Your vivacious and positive spirit is an inspiration. Thank you for your friendship. I wish to thank David who assisted me in some of my financial divorce details. Thank you for treating me with respect and dignity. I appreciate your values and integrity. I wish to thank my clients for continuing to trust me, always, with my expertise and care during my divorce and always. Thank you Margaret for your continued friendship and support in all that I do. Thank you, Angie, for trusting my vision and being my cheerleader. You have been there for more than one project. Thank you for your friendship. I have enjoyed sharing personal growth with you. Thank you Carol, my memoir teacher, for providing carefully delivered feedback. It was much appreciated. Thank you, Jessica, for your synergy and for listening to my wine-theme vision and embracing it, which gave me the courage to go with it. Your input is appreciated. Thank you Randy and Pegotty Cooper of CDC College for Divorce Coaching ™ for your certification program that further developed my skills to work with clients to empower them to take action, shift perspective, and co-create solutions to achieve desired results. Coaching skills are a powerful tool that I will embrace to enhance the quality of all my relationships. www.certifieddivorcecoach.com. A special thanks to Jerry Cohen, CPA, CDFA that educated me on divorce financial planning who can be reached at www.californiadivorcefinancialplanning.com. Heartfelt thanks to

Debra Oakland who read my manuscript and contributed her writing on courage. You are an inspiration to all with your courageous spirit. Visit Debra at www.livingincourageonline.com.

CDC CERTIFIED DIVORCE COACH

Why hire a divorce coach? So you don't have to get divorced alone! You'll have a partner to help guide you through the process of divorce. There are different approaches to divorce coaching. As a Meritage Divorce Coach, my philosophy is to assist the client in identifying the appropriate divorce support system to meet their specific needs, goals, and objectives. Your divorce is only as good as your divorce support system. Engaging the right professionals, and taking care of your physical, emotional, and spiritual needs will offer the best possible outcome. Every effort is made to streamline the divorce process and break it down into less overwhelming steps. The more prepared you are to sit in front of your hired professionals to focus on what they do best, the less money you will spend in broader ranges of concerns. By helping a client engage efficiently, a divorce coach can greatly reduce the cost of divorce.

My clients are also given the opportunity to embark on the Meritage Divorce Journey and embrace the "barrel refinement process" of transformation with guided self-reflection exercises. As a Meritage Divorce Coach, I will look inside your barrel and make sure you are still in there, or at the very least, still decanting. The Meritage Divorce Journey guides you in identifying a winemaking formula to re-produce yourself. You'll develop ways to spit out the past, re-produce yourself, and decant a future. In the role of Divorce Coach, I act as your assistant winemaker, guide, sounding board, and barrel-refinement-process facilitator. My passion and goal is to help deliver a better version of you on the other side of the journey, wearing your own pair of wine-colored glasses—and able to see with better clarity!

As a CDC, Certified Divorce Coach, I am held to the highest level of confidentiality and ethics, and professionally trained by top coaches in coaching principles. I assist in the co-creation of client-generated solutions and strategies.

With God and a Divorce Coach, and yourself, you really aren't alone. Sorry, we can't be drinking buddies, but we can share perspectives and the essence of our wine-selves.

Dear Wine Friend:

Thank you for allowing me to share in your divorce journey and for supporting my work. It is my hope that, at the very least, you didn't feel completely alone.

I'd love to hear from you. Please stop by the Meritage Divorce website www.meritagedivorce.com where you can also read and comment on the blog, share your divorce stories, and send me an email. You'll find additional resources and information on our Meritage Divorce Journey workshops held in various locations.

Meritage Divorce is a registered trademark. All rights reserved.

P.O. Box 27, Newport Beach, CA 92662

Cheryl Nielsen

Cheryl Nielsen is a CDC Certified Divorce Coach™ and Meritage Divorce Journey workshop presenter. She is passionate about coaching others through the experience of divorce to re-align with their authentic selves and identify the underlying spiritual lessons to provide an opportunity to heal, grow, and live a more fulfilling life. She combines her coaching skills, personal wisdom, vineyard experience, and love for wine to assist clients in becoming "re-produced." She writes in wine metaphors and analogies to provide entertainment value for the wine lover.

Transforming lives and creating a unique and memorable experience for others is her underlying passion. She also enjoys spending time with her dog Stubbs, cooking, outdoor activities, and trips to Napa and the local farmer's market.

Married in 1995, and divorced in 2009